FELIX NOBIS is a poet, playwright, and actor. He was playwright-in-residence with the Q Theatre (Penrith, NSW); and was a member of the Sydney Theatre Company's Fresh Ink program and Melbourne Theatre Company's Affiliate Writers' program. He is currently a lecturer with the Centre for Theatre and Performance at Monash University.

As a poet and performer, Felix has toured his translation of the medieval epic poem, *Beowulf*, as a one-person show throughout the US and Europe. He also adapted and narrated the translation for ABC Radio National's 'Poetica' program. His one-person poetical narrative, *Once Upon a Barstool*, was commissioned by An Chomhairle Ealaíon (Arts Council of Ireland). It premiered in Cork, Ireland before enjoying a successful season at La Mama Theatre and a tour of regional Victoria in 2009.

Felix has worked extensively with ABC Radio National as a performer and occasional producer. He has worked with ABC TV as an actor in series such as 'Janus' and 'MDA'. Felix is an award-winning poet. In 2014 a selection of his poetry was recorded and CD-released as a volume of *Going Down Swinging*'s 'One Night Wonders' series.

Matthew Dyktynski (left) as Gordon and Martin Blum as Hunter in Larrikin Ensemble Theatre Productions' 2013 production at fortyfivedownstairs, Melbourne. (Photo: Sarah Walker)

BOY OUT OF THE COUNTRY

FELIX NOBIS

Currency Press, Sydney

CURRENCY PLAYS

First published in 2016
by Currency Press Pty Ltd,
PO Box 2287, Strawberry Hills, NSW, 2012, Australia
enquiries@currency.com.au
www.currency.com.au

Cataloguing-in-publication data for this title is available from the National Library of Australia website: www.nla.gov.au

Typeset by Dean Nottle for Currency Press.
Cover design by Katy Wall.
Front cover background image by redwolf518stock.
Front cover shows Martin Blum (left) as Hunter and Matthew Dyktynski as Gordon in Larrikin Ensemble Theatre Productions' 2013 production at fortyfivedownstairs, Melbourne. (Photo: Sarah Walker)

Currency Press acknowledges the Traditional Owners of the Country on which we live and work. We pay our respects to all Aboriginal and Torres Strait Islander Elders, past and present.

Contents

*Jane Clifton as Margaret in Larrikin Ensemble Theatre Productions'
2013 production at fortyfivedownstairs, Melbourne. (Photo: Sarah Walker)*

INTRODUCTION

I am a boy out of the country. I have one brother; we had our mythical places of adventure; we made model aeroplanes—but let's stop there. I don't yet want to give away too much of this marvellous play, and how it connects with my own history.

I connect to this play—and I invite you to connect to it, too—because it speaks to the present as much as it does to the past. For someone like me, who teaches two rarely-intersecting dramatic traditions (Australian and Shakespearean), *Boy Out of the Country* is gold dust. This play tackles some of the staples of Australian drama: the country's impact on its people; the peoples' impact on the country; men behaving like boys and the women who put up with them (or not); love and sex; past and present. This is a play very much about inheritance. In this, *Boy Out of the Country* shares kinship with the Australian dramatic staple, Ray Lawler's *Summer of the Seventeenth Doll*. Like Lawler, Nobis engages in a Shakespearian revelry in language: glorious, idiomatic, rhythmical, muscular, and hilariously bad language. Rarely has the word 'fuck' been rendered so poetic. The prologue suggests this language should be 'celebrated rather than shied away from', and spoken aloud. I agree. Take some companions and a few copies of this book, go to a somewhat removed paddock, and let it rip!

Let me offer you some of the production history of *Boy Out of the Country*. I first heard the play in a development reading at fortyfivedownstairs, Melbourne. I descended a couple of flights of stairs and emerged—greeted by Melbourne's most ebullient front-of-housers—into a timber-floored and paint-flecked warehouse. Five actors sat onstage in a row, and stood in turn to speak their lines. I was spellbound. Sixty years ago, the first audiences of *The Doll* reported that the play made them feel spoken for, spoken to, spoken through. These were my feelings at *Boy*. The pace, the rhythm, the force of the language: five somewhat under-prepared actors were belting out this play-poem and it was as visceral as the footy finals.

I wondered about the play being staged as a full production, and felt slightly apprehensive that its dynamism might be reduced when the actors moved around and physically represented the action. The direct address of a development reading suits the play. It contains beautifully interwoven scenes of—yes, Shakespeare or Monk O'Neill-like—direct address to the audience. It could easily be a radio play. Could it be a film, too? A film in Aussie verse? I needn't have worried about a full staging. The 2013 production was as funny and nuanced as one could hope for. But that first, intimate, privileged development reading: 'tis in my memory locked. (Parenthetical suggestions: 1. Go to developments readings, they might just be magical; 2. Try reading this play aloud with characters seated in a row; let the rhythms sink deep.)

One little note on Etho. Etho is the grand, mythical place where *Boy*'s brothers, Hunter and Gordon, find adventure. My brother and I had a place just like it—though we didn't have a name for it. Our place contained a dam, mullock heaps, rabbits, snakes, a raft, tunnels, and a summer's worth of mischief. Perhaps you won't connect to this play quite as personally as I do. But great drama offers connections to worlds distant as well as close; inconceivable as well as familiar. If you've not yet journeyed to an Etho, turn the page … enjoy.

Rob Conkie
Melbourne
January 2016

Rob Conkie is a Senior Lecturer of Theatre and Drama at LaTrobe University.

ACKNOWLEDGEMENTS

Some people get mentioned a great deal in theatre acknowledgements. Julian Meyrick and Mary Lou Jelbart are two such people, and like many before me, I extend my thanks to them. Julian nurtured this work as part of Melbourne Theatre Company's Affiliate Writers' program, and Mary Lou supported the play through its rehearsed reading stages to the successful season at fortyfivedownstairs. True champions of theatre should be celebrated at every opportunity.

I extend my thanks to the many actors who have been part of the development of this script, particularly Ezra Bix, Geoff Lemon, Alison Richards, Drew Tingwell and others who gave their character insights over the play's long gestation. I particularly thank the cast of the fortyfivedownstairs production and all who were involved that season, especially co-director Fleur Kilpatrick.

I also express my gratitude for the support of the R. E. Ross Trust, Monash Academy of Performing Arts, and our major production sponsor Jayco. My thanks go to Rob Conkie and Currency Press, especially Claire Grady and Stefania Cox. Thanks to Monash University for their ongoing support. Finally, I extend my thanks to my siblings and friends, many of whom appear in this play in one form or another, and to my partner Ben for his support throughout.

The play is dedicated to Greg Smeaton (1958–2013) a great story-teller; and to my mother, who knew how to raise boys.

Felix Nobis

Chris Bunworth as Sergeant Walker in Larrikin Ensemble Theatre Productions' 2013 production at fortyfivedownstairs, Melbourne. (Photo: Sarah Walker)

Boy Out of the Country was originally produced by Wolf Heidecker / Larrikin Ensemble Theatre at fortyfivedownstairs, Melbourne, on 21 November 2013, with the following cast:

HUNTER	Martin Blum
GORDON	Matthew Dyktynski
RACHEL	Amanda LaBonte
MARGARET	Jane Clifton
SERGEANT WALKER	Chris Bunworth

Directors, Fleur Kilpatrick & Felix Nobis
Designer, Rob Sowinski
Dramaturg, Julian Meyrick
Original Music, Bang Mango Cools

CHARACTERS

HUNTER SMEATON, in his 40s

GORDON SMEATON, Hunter's older brother, in his 40s

RACHEL SMEATON, married to Gordon

MARGARET SMEATON, mother of Hunter and Gordon

SERGEANT WALKER, the local cop, 58

SETTING

The action of the play takes place in Cradletown, a small country town in regional Victoria.

A NOTE ON THE LANGUAGE

This play is in verse. The verse is not always apparent within the written text and should rarely be obvious in performance, yet every section engages with poetic structures of metre, rhythm and occasionally rhyme. I encourage the reader to speak some passages out loud and to find the rhythm within the scene ... I encourage the actors to fight against the rhythm once it is found and to speak the language as their own. The audience should find something natural and yet strange about the language, and this is the desired effect.

Whereas the play contains a fair amount of bad language, a close reading will reveal that the swearing actually consists almost entirely of the same word repeated over and over. This word is employed to emphasise rhythm, humour and often propels the language forward. In this, it contributes a poetic, rather than vulgar tone to the play, and should be celebrated rather than shied away from.

ACT ONE

SCENE ONE

A country police station.

GORDON *enters, holding a handkerchief to his busted eye. He is
followed immediately by* HUNTER *and then* SERGEANT WALKER. *An
argument is in full swing.*

GORDON:	Why?!
HUNTER:	What d'ya mean / 'Why'?
WALKER:	/ Oh, for God's sake, Hunter. *Why?!*
HUNTER:	Why not ask why Gordon keeps his mother in a cupboard?
GORDON:	Why not ask why Hunter, after seven years of silence wants to—
HUNTER:	Why not ask why Gordon—? And it wasn't even seven—
GORDON:	After seven solid years of total silence—
HUNTER:	Wants to lock up his poor mother, And I sent a dozen postcards.
GORDON:	Not to me!
HUNTER:	No, not to you! As if I'd send a fucking postcard to you, ya dumb shit!
GORDON:	Simply turns up out of nowhere, and [*touching his eye*] ouch! Jesus!
HUNTER:	Have you seen this place?
WALKER:	No.
HUNTER:	It's a refrigerator. Dirty lino on the floor—
WALKER:	Although—
HUNTER:	It's cold, dark, small, it's pretty much a Kelvinator.
WALKER:	Though—

HUNTER:	The difference is no light goes on, when you open up the door!
WALKER:	Although—
GORDON:	I'll have you know, *she* chose it, and *she's* happy there!
WALKER:	I've heard—
GORDON:	It *costs*, I don't mind saying—
HUNTER:	Gordon, I don't want to hear!
GORDON:	Well, you're not paying it!
	It costs almost thirty grand a year!
HUNTER:	As if *you* pay, As if *you* pay!
WALKER:	Hey, hey, hey, hey,
	Hey, hey, hey, hey!

Silence.

Now, both of yuz … Just … Both of yuz, just …
Both sit down!
The amount of times I've pulled you both apart like dogs
in the street,
Your poor mother!
If you have no respect for yourselves …
Your poor mother!
I get a phone call from the Golden Crown, 'The Smeaton
boys are back at it'.
How long have the pair of ya been back in the same
town, eh?
'The Smeaton boys are back at it!'

I remember your old man, draggin' the pair of yuz,
Kickin' and screamin', by your torn school clothes,
Your poor mother was crying,
And two of yuz tryin' to kill each other,
Throws ya down and gets the garden hose.
And don't go thinkin', for a moment, that I won't do the
same.
Shame is all I can say, shame bloody shame on yuz.
What kinda yahoos are yuz, eh?
…

GORDON: I—

WALKER: Now, Hunter! I hear this home your mum's at is okay.
           Although I ain't personally seen it.

GORDON: She gets two hot meals a day!

WALKER: Gordon, I *mean it*, mate!
           You'll both get your say.
           But for the moment, I just wanna hear from Hunter.

HUNTER: Hear what?

WALKER: Welcome back. You're looking well.
           How ya been? And what the fuckin' hell is going on here
           son?

HUNTER: Dunno whatcha mean.

WALKER: What brings ya back to town?
           When did you get it in?
           How long you plan to stick around?

GORDON: And—

WALKER: Gordon! Why don't you and I just listen for a
               moment?
           Hear what Hunter's got to say.

GORDON: I want to talk to Rachel.

WALKER: She's already on her way.
           Now … Hunter?

HUNTER: Alf?

           …
           Whatcha wanna know?

WALKER: How long you plan to stay?

HUNTER: Dunno, maybe a day or so.

WALKER: When did ya get in?

HUNTER: Turned up this arvo, eh.

WALKER: Drove?

HUNTER: By bus.

WALKER: From where?

HUNTER: Ballarat.

GORDON: Is *that* where you've been hiding?

HUNTER:	No, it's where I caught a bus, ya fuckin' nong.
WALKER:	And then?
HUNTER:	Stopped in at the Crown.
	Had a few pots,
	No-one I knew there so I went to visit Mum.
WALKER:	I see. Was she expecting you?
HUNTER:	Not that I know of.
WALKER:	But it's the first time you've seen her, for what? For how long?
HUNTER:	A couple of years? I don't know. I been away.
GORDON:	You been away?! *He's been away!*
	We fuckin' hadn't noticed, eh?
WALKER:	Alright, / Gordon
GORDON:	/ Seven years of peace. We never would have noticed!
WALKER:	Go on, Hunter.
HUNTER:	Turned up at the old place. All fenced off.
	Fuckin' padlock on the door. Graffiti and stuff
	All over the place: a war zone.
	You been there lately?
	Steps and porch all overgrown
	With weeds and crap,
	And these kids hangin' around on pushbikes.
	I go, 'Mrs Smeaton who lives here, you know where she is?'
	And one of these little fucks is like,
	Yeah, he does, but it'll cost me ten bucks,
	And I grab him, and tell him, I'll ask you again,
	'N' if you don't want that pushbike shoved up your arse you can
	Tell me what you know.
	By which time his old man rocks up
	Waving a three-o-fuckin'-three,
	And guess who it was?
	…

              Owen Flasher Henderson!
              Who showed his dick to that fifth-class chick in high
              school, you remember?
              Tells me Mum's moved twenty k,
              Up toward Talley, but he's headin' out that way,
              And he can give me a lift.
              Shifty little ten-dollar mafia tacker in the backa the ute,
              And off we fuckin' go.
              And guess what he tells me next?

GORDON: That—

HUNTER: That the place has been empty for about six months,
              But now, apparently, some bastard wants
              To buy it as part of some kinda *housing development!*

GORDON: Let me explain.

HUNTER: By which time we're there!
              Beetlewood, overgrown,
              Broken down, fuckin' aged care home
              In the arse end of nowhere.
              Mum's in the twilight zone.
              Dressing-gown in the middle of the afternoon,
              Sittin' in solitary confinement, in her pokey fuckin' fridge.
              Sleeping through the day, no idea who's who.

GORDON: Well, ya been away for seven years, as if she's gonna
              know you!

HUNTER: Kicked out of her house—

GORDON: That's a—

HUNTER: Stuck into a home.

GORDON: A lie!

HUNTER: Doped up on morphine!

GORDON: Crap!

HUNTER: And left out there to die!

GORDON: Now just—

HUNTER: And what I want to know is, if the property's getting sold
              For some kinda *housing development*,
              And if what Flasher Henderson told me's all true,

	Then there's something, Gordon,
	Accordin' to him,
	In the area of one million dollars,
	Maybe even two!
GORDON:	Oh, here we go! Here we go!
HUNTER:	And what I want to know is—
GORDON:	If that's all you're after.
HUNTER:	It's not what I'm after—
GORDON:	Let's just get one thing clear—
HUNTER:	But I spoke to Mum, mate, and I fuckin' *asked her*.
	And it turns out she's got no bloody *idea*
	About a *housing development!*
	In fact, and get this, as far as she knows,
	She signed the place over,
	And everything goes to you and your family!
	Now just explain that!
GORDON:	That's Mum getting old,
	That's just basically not true.
HUNTER:	So you're saying that she lied?
GORDON:	What I'm saying, Hunter, is that I'd
	Be very careful about making accusations, if I were you,
	Before checking your facts.
WALKER:	Alright, boys.
GORDON:	Can we get one thing clear?
	Nothing unusual or untoward is going on around here.
	Alright?
	Don't start thinking you've uncovered some murky affair
	Because the only thing uncovered here is life, Hunter,
	Just life.
	Just grown-ups living life.
	Mum simply got too old, and the place was too big for
	her alone.
	Sooner or later it was gonna have to be sold.
	Now, as it turns out, the property's situated
	In a recently enabled council subdivision zone—
WALKER:	For building housing estates.

GORDON: Dad's will clearly states
That the land goes to his children *and his grandchildren.*
And up until now, as far as anybody knew,
And correct me if I'm wrong, but there were only *two* grandchildren,
My two girls, Coralie and Gracie.
Now nothing in the world is going to stop this housing estate,
So naturally, on behalf of both of them, I've been trying to negotiate
The best possible price.

HUNTER: So it's fuckin' true!

GORDON: Okay, you know what? I don't have to explain anything further to you!
I'm acting on behalf of *three* beneficiaries,
It would have been remiss of me
Not to get the best possible deal.

I know it's where we grew up, Hunter,
I know how you must feel,
But the opportunity arose and I had to decide fast
…
Between giving my girls a future,
Or hanging on to some relic of the past.
And as for Mum, she got too old, and she simply couldn't stay.

RACHEL *has entered.*

RACHEL: Hello, sergeant.

WALKER: Hello, Rachel!

GORDON: Sweetheart!

RACHEL: Hello, Gordon … Hunter.

Pause. HUNTER *and* RACHEL *look at each other.*

HUNTER: You're lookin' well.

RACHEL: Really? That's all you've got to say?

HUNTER *and* RACHEL *are still looking at each other.*

GORDON: *Look at my eye!*
RACHEL: What happened, sweetheart?
GORDON: I was drinking at the Golden Crown—
RACHEL: Look up.
GORDON: He barges in—
RACHEL: And down.
GORDON: He's lucky I don't press charges—
RACHEL: Up.
GORDON: I leave the bar and turn around.
WALKER: Hunter struck at Gordon.
GORDON: Holding three pots and a pony!
WALKER: No apparent provocation.
GORDON: Christ, he's only just got back after all these years away,
          He just turns up out of nowhere.

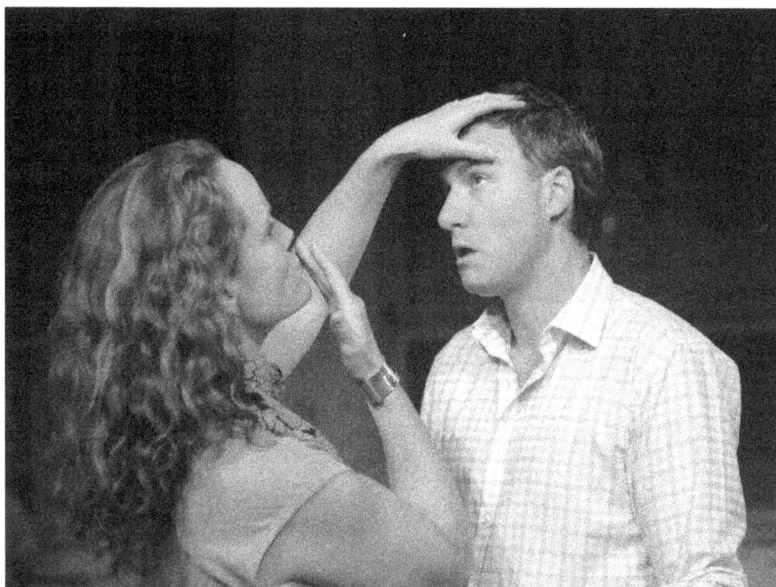

Amanda LaBonte as Rachel and Matthew Dyktynski as Gordon in Larrikin Ensemble Theatre Productions' 2013 production at fortyfivedownstairs, Melbourne. (Photo: Sarah Walker)

HUNTER: Oh, I got plenty to say.

RACHEL: Really?

GORDON: Rachel? I go to put the drinks down for a brotherly
embrace,
And guess what he does?

There is a pause. RACHEL *and* HUNTER *are looking at each
other.*

WALKER: [*helpfully*] He hit Gordon in the face.

RACHEL: I can see that, sergeant, thank you.

WALKER: Well.

RACHEL: Just tell me what I have to do,
It's the middle of the afternoon,
Gracie's got violin at two,
They've both got their eisteddfods soon.
Is Gordon free to go or …?

WALKER: Let him off with a caution.

GORDON: My things are at the pub.

RACHEL: Well, unfortunately, Gordon,
You'll have to pick up Gracie,
Because Coralie's got Little Athletics at three,
And I've only got the big car,
So you'll have to drop off Coralie and me
At the oval before you go.
Hunter? Where are you staying?

HUNTER: Uhm, I don't really—

GORDON: I don't really think so.

RACHEL: We've got four spare rooms, Gordon,
There's no point your brother paying good money to that
awful motel.

Pause.

HUNTER: I'll get a room at the pub.

RACHEL: Suit yourself. The offer stands. Any time.
Doesn't it, Gordon?
Give you both a chance to speak

	Instead of yelling at each other. I could hear you halfway up the street.
GORDON:	I was trying to explain—
RACHEL:	Gordon, invite your brother Over for dinner tonight. …
GORDON:	I'm not really sure if—
RACHEL:	Hunter?
HUNTER:	I don't know … Alright.
RACHEL:	A chance to let your nieces find out who on earth you are, After all these years.
GORDON:	He just walks into the bloody bar—
RACHEL:	A chance for us to catch up and to see how things have changed.
GORDON:	He just turns up out of nowhere, Rache, And stands there like a deranged bloody—
WALKER:	You know what, Rachel's right, Both of ya could use a little time to talk things through.
RACHEL:	So that's settled. You're invited to a barbecue at our place tonight, Hunter. Now, both of you shake hands. And apologise to the sergeant, Though I'm sure he understands What the two of you are like.
WALKER:	Of course I bloody do! Jesus, I remember one night—
RACHEL:	Maybe next time, sergeant, thank you. Now shake … We have to get the girls from school. Hunter, put your hand out, and Gordon, you'll—
GORDON:	Alright! Sweetheart, we know how to shake hands. …
HUNTER:	I'm sorry about your eye.
GORDON:	I'm sorry about your face.
HUNTER:	Ha fuckin' ha.

They shake.

GORDON: So we see you around our place for a barbecue tonight?

RACHEL: There's the address, Hunter,
            The girls go to bed at eight.
            [*Sternly*] Stay sober until then.

GORDON: Oh, and Hunter, mate.

HUNTER: Yeah?

GORDON: Good to see you again.

They go.

WALKER: My arse!
            He's as happy to see you as a warm parcel of shit on a
            hot day.

HUNTER: Why you say that?

WALKER: Especially right now.
            You want a beer?

HUNTER: Might as well.

WALKER: Might as well while you're here, eh?

HUNTER: So why you say that?

WALKER: What? Never said nothin', mate.

WALKER *gets two beers from a small fridge behind the station
counter.*

            There ya go.

HUNTER: Ta.

WALKER: So, tell me Hunter, where you been?

HUNTER: Up north.

WALKER: Uhuh. Staying out of trouble?

HUNTER: Yeah, 'course.
            Just workin' on the rigs.

WALKER: Not what I heard.

HUNTER: You heard wrong.

WALKER: Because I don't want any kinda—

HUNTER: You heard wrong.

            …

WALKER: So, nothing I should know.

HUNTER: Nothing I can think of.

WALKER: And I'm supposed to—

HUNTER: Cheers, big ears.

WALKER: Up your bum.
            I'm supposed to believe you're just back here for a day?

HUNTER: Might be, I dunno.
            Sometimes these things are hard to say.

WALKER: So what, maybe a week or so?

HUNTER: I can't say for sure.

WALKER: A couple of weeks?

HUNTER: I dunno.

WALKER: A month, ya reckon?
            Less? More?

HUNTER: Have to wait and see.

WALKER: Because it suddenly seems old Cradletown is *quite the
            fuckin' place to be.*

HUNTER: Is that a fact?

WALKER: So it would seem!
            'Course, you'd have to ask your brother.
            But who'd a dreamed, twenty years ago,
            That we'd be talking *real estate*, in Cradletown?

HUNTER: Real estate?

WALKER: Talking fuckin' *real estate*, in Cradletown!
            Everybody's on about some property or another.

HUNTER: Like Mum's place, you mean?

WALKER: Well, you'd have to ask your brother about that, eh?
            He's a fuckin' clever bugger when it comes to real estate.
            …

HUNTER: So—

WALKER: You hear they're tearin' down this lockup?

HUNTER: Yeah?

WALKER: After all this time.
            Building a *regional police station* out in Talley.

Lots of talk at the moment about prime location,
And 'catchment area'. You know what that is?

HUNTER: Catchment area?

WALKER: Catching people, people catchment.
Catchment of young families.
It's all catchment and location,
And growth fuckin' corridor,
But I'll tell you one thing, Hunter,
I'll tell you one thing right now,
Nobody talks about the *land* anymore.
Have a little listen when you're walking around town,
It's all properties this and investments that
And interest rates going up and down,
And one minute it's all a pile of worthless shithouse
land,
And the next minute, it's *real estate*,
And worth five hundred fuckin' grand.

HUNTER: So all that stuff is true?

WALKER: Here's something you don't know,
Local population? Estimated to grow *over forty-two
percent*
Within the next two years.

HUNTER: Forty-two percent?!

WALKER: Now when you were born, or your brother,
I sent your mother flowers,
I bought your dad a beer,
And that's the way the population used to increase
around here.
One little kiddie at a time.
And now they're tearing down this holding cell,
A bunch of suits and ties are supposed to tell us all what
to do.

HUNTER: *Forty-two percent?!*

WALKER: Mate, I remember, you spent a night in here or two.
You and your brother!

The fuckin' pair of you.
I had Gordon in here once.

HUNTER: I know.

WALKER: Another fuckin' fight.

HUNTER: I know.

WALKER: *You* got away, but I put your bloody brother in that cell there for the night,
As much to give your mum a break,
As give you little shits a fright.
I get back in the morning, and somebody … *some*body—

HUNTER: It wasn't me.

WALKER: But *some*body had hotwired the bulldozer, security lock and all,
From the old council compound,
And knocked down that fucking wall over there!

HUNTER: It wasn't me.

WALKER: The great escape!
…
Amount of fuckin' paperwork that put me through.

HUNTER: I wouldn't know.

WALKER: I'll tell you something though, haven't told you this before.
The night I put him in here?
Didn't even lock the fuckin' door.

HUNTER: Ya jokin'?

WALKER: Serious.

HUNTER: And the whole wall came down!

WALKER: I come in, in the morning, it's a pile of stone and rubble,
And he coulda walked out the front door,
Saved us all the fuckin' trouble in the world.

HUNTER: Ha!

WALKER: Ha ha ha ha!

HUNTER: Ha ha ha ha!

They laugh. Then silence. They drink their beer and look around.

WALKER:	Long fuckin' time ago now. This time she's comin' down for real. God only knows how I'm supposed to feel about that. *Regional police station.* Fifteen blocks of new estates 'n' Forty-two percent increase in population Over the next two years.
HUNTER:	How many blocks ya reckon?
WALKER:	Fifteen to start. All built on spec 'n' Then twice that again once they sell.
HUNTER:	Where the hell they plan to put all that?
WALKER:	Ain't that just the question. Somewhere with a lot of space.
HUNTER:	Like …
WALKER:	The old orchards out by Jacobs'. Those smaller blocks out down the back of your old place.
HUNTER:	But our whole property only takes in five acres.
WALKER:	Not just your old property, mate. This bloody new estate is Gonna stretch right up to the railway tracks! Starts at your old place but backs on to the dams, Takes in the orchards and the ruins down by the old mine, Stretches all the way across, Bloody right up to the railway line.
HUNTER:	But half that land's council-owned.
WALKER:	Been bought up by investors, mate, and quietly re-zoned Over the last few months.
HUNTER:	No way!
WALKER:	There's some poor buggers hanging on. Some good people wanna stay!
HUNTER:	All that bloody land we used to play when we were kids?
WALKER:	Been bought up by investors, mate. Be worth a fair few quid since those days, I reckon. Sale pending next few months, but pretty much agreed. Sad times that you've walked into, Hunter. Sad bloody times indeed.

HUNTER: Christ!

WALKER: You boys even had a name for it, all those years ago?
           I think? Didn't ya?
           You used to call it … What did you used to call it?

HUNTER: We used to call it Etho.

WALKER: Etho! Ha! There ya fuckin' go.

HUNTER: So what kinda investors are they?
           They from outa town?

WALKER: How's your drink there, mate?

HUNTER: Alf? … Have ya found that out?
           Do ya know?

WALKER: How's your drink? Are you ready for another?

           WALKER *goes for two more beers.*

HUNTER: Or are they local?

WALKER: All I was saying was that … he's a clever man, your
           brother.
           …

HUNTER: That bastard.

           HUNTER *goes.*

WALKER: Now don't go reading too much into it!
           And you heard nothing from me!
           All I'm sayin' is these suits and ties
           Have their fat fuckin' fingers in a lot of grubby pies,
           If you know what I mean.
           Hey, Hunter, where ya goin'?!
           I didn't mean nothin'!
           Just the population's growin' faster than fuckin' locusts!
           And while some are getting rich in this mongrel town,
           The rest of us are watching our lockups pulled down
           And getting trampled into the dry fuckin' ground,
           And left behind, that's all I meant!
           Population increase fuckin' forty-two percent,
           What the *hell* do they all want here?!
           Hoons and refugees and Africans and queers
           Fillin' up the joint!

Come on, Hunter, you understand!
…
Let's talk about the old days, mate!
…
Let's talk about the land.

SCENE TWO

HUNTER *and* GORDON *speak directly to the audience.*

HUNTER: Used to be this land, out back of our old place
            That we used to muck around in as kids.
            And one day we decided it needed a name.
GORDON: You decided.
HUNTER: Gordon was really the brains behind the operation back
            then.
GORDON: Ha fuckin' ha.
HUNTER: And he was supposed to find a name that meant, you
            know, 'Paradise'.
GORDON: We couldn't have called it 'Paradise'.
HUNTER: No, that was a bit *too* lame, even for Gordon.
GORDON: So I asked Mrs Lambert.
HUNTER: Gordon asked a teacher.
GORDON: And she said this word 'Utopia',
            Which meant idyllic—
HUNTER: —kind of—
GORDON: —perfect place.
HUNTER: Like Etho.
GORDON: Like Etho was.
HUNTER: Open space.
            Fruit trees used to grow in these old orchards,
            And we'd just go there, pretty much each arvo.
GORDON: These two old dams, and we built a raft.
HUNTER: And it fuckin' sank.
GORDON: And we fuckin' laughed
            For ages, didn't we?

HUNTER:	For ages, Watching it go down.
GORDON:	Footy-sock flag, flapping, as it's sinking under water.
HUNTER:	And no-one used to go there.
GORDON:	Just us.
HUNTER:	Just the two of us, and we pretty much sorta Owned the place really. Miles and miles.
GORDON:	And then the weekend came to name it And we had this ceremony all worked out.
HUNTER:	The two of us, quite serious.
GORDON:	We got a stick.
HUNTER:	We had a staff, and we put our hands on it, and we both swore—
GORDON:	We swore—
HUNTER:	Forever to be protectors of 'Utopia'. Remember?
GORDON:	Yeah, we did. … But this was all in the seventies, right, back when we were kids, And the thing is, you see, that around the time of the naming of Utopia, … It happened, that *Ethiopia* was very much in the news.
HUNTER:	Because of the famine and the drought.
GORDON:	And somehow—
HUNTER:	Somehow—
GORDON:	These two names …
HUNTER:	Kinda got confused in our little brains.
GORDON:	And with all solemn ceremony, We declared our paradise place of lakes and trees And plentiful fruits of every sort To be christened *'Ethiopia'*. …

HUNTER:	'Etho' for short.
GORDON:	And, once it was named.
HUNTER:	Well, Etho it remained.
GORDON:	Forever.
HUNTER:	Forever … Or so we fuckin' thought.

SCENE THREE

Margaret's unit.

MARGARET *is in her dressing-gown watching the TV.* HUNTER *is in the kitchenette making tea.*

HUNTER:	Sugar, Mum?
TV:	Twenty-four … eighteen
HUNTER:	Mum? Sugar?
TV:	And the supplementary: nine.
HUNTER:	*Mum, do you want sugar in your tea?!*
MARGARET:	[*turning the TV off*] Stop yelling! I've been living here six months and I've been perfectly fine Without you messing up my kitchen, or carrying on with flowers. If you're going to make tea, Graham, make a pot. And don't use the Lan-Choo teabags either Use the ones—
HUNTER:	Fuckin' hell, Mum, do you want sugar or not?
MARGARET:	I'll sugar you! I don't want sugar, or tea, if that's the tone you're going to use. I don't know what you think you're doing, you turn up here at all hours.
HUNTER:	It was midday, Mum.
MARGARET:	And I was having my midday snooze! You scared the life out of me, Graham.
HUNTER:	Can you just stop calling me Graham.
MARGARET:	Well, *excuse me*, Graham! But I think I know your name.

HUNTER: Nobody's called me that for ages.

MARGARET: Your father was a Graham.

HUNTER: My father was an arsehole.

MARGARET: But a Graham, all the same.

                …

HUNTER: Everybody calls me Hunter.

MARGARET: Everybody but your mother.
              If I started with the nicknames I'd be calling your brother
              'Bucket'.

HUNTER: Ha! We used to call him Bucket!

MARGARET: And you gave him one for Christmas,
              And when he unwrapped it, the poor boy was in tears.
              He was so disappointed, you ruined his Christmas,
              And then you kept it up for the next five years.
              You were a wicked little brother.

HUNTER: I suppose I really was.

MARGARET: I used to think you'd kill each other.

HUNTER: Here's your tea, Mum. White with three.

MARGARET: *I just told you no sugar!*

HUNTER: *I'm joking, Mum, Jesus.*

MARGARET: You're a fool of a boy!

HUNTER: Absolutely, Mum, that's me.

                …

              So, you're happy here, you reckon, yeah?

MARGARET: I've already told you.

HUNTER: Just seems sorta dark, that's all. Seems sorta cold.
              I can feel a kinda draft coming in from somewhere.
              You oughta be careful.

MARGARET: Maybe you're just getting old, Graham. Take a blanket.

HUNTER: Ya reckon?
              Does Gordon take a blanket when he comes around to
              visit?
              Or the girls, when they come around to Grandma's house
              to play?

MARGARET: Everybody's busy.

HUNTER: But it isn't that hard, is it?
             I mean I've been here twice in the same fuckin' day,
             And when's the last time they—
MARGARET: Language!
HUNTER: —the girls came to visit?

MARGARET looks away.

             Mum?
MARGARET: What?
HUNTER: When's the last time the girls … You're not serious.
             They've never even been here?
MARGARET: Besides, you're one to talk!
HUNTER: How could I visit? I was two thousand miles away,
             Thirty k offshore.
MARGARET: Everybody's busy.
HUNTER: And I sent ya coupla postcards.
MARGARET: Well, nobody lives at that old address anymore.
HUNTER: No, Mum, I know …
             So, do you miss it?
MARGARET: That's enough out of you. Sit down and drink your tea!
HUNTER: All I was asking—
MARGARET: I know exactly what you're saying!
             And your brother's been a very good son to me.
HUNTER: Mum.
MARGARET: He pays for this flat.
HUNTER: Yeah? And why'd you think he might do that?
             You know you're only in here 'cause he wants you off
             that land.
             Do you know how much he could sell it for?
MARGARET: It isn't worth much anymore. It's a weatherboard,
             Graham.
HUNTER: Christ, you really don't understand, do you?
MARGARET: How anyone just disappears?
             Without a word? For seven years?
             As if nobody's ever heard of a telephone? No!
             And then you just start making tea,

	Accusing Gordon, blaming me,
	Because he tried to put some kind of plans in place while you were gone?
	You were gone!
HUNTER:	Mum.
MARGARET:	Your father left the land to his children and his grandchildren.
HUNTER:	That's—
MARGARET:	And don't you even try to tell me that it isn't fair!
	Goodness, boy, who could tell if you were in hospital or hell,
	And this way, I thought at least the two girls get their share,
	And I swear that's all I thought of.
HUNTER:	Was it Gordon's idea?
MARGARET:	… Sort of.
HUNTER:	Jesus!
MARGARET:	He was trying—
HUNTER:	No, he wasn't. Don't you see?
	He kicked you out of your house!
MARGARET:	I was alone. It was confusing! Nobody came to visit,
	And then this place became free.
HUNTER:	Well, this place is a shithole, half of these are standing empty.
MARGARET:	*And what should I have done?!*
	I couldn't stay there on my own.
	At least Gordon would telephone each Sunday afternoon,
	And I'd speak to the girls,
	And then watch a bit of SBS before they had those terrible commercials.
	I'd make myself a little pot of Sunday stew,
	And watch a film, Dutch or Swedish,
	I don't know. Something strange.
	And there was one about an old woman who lived on her own …
HUNTER:	Mum …

MARGARET: Except that she couldn't pay her rent,
And all of her neighbours wanted her gone,
But then, one day, she accidently went
And burnt something on her stove,
And her stove looked just like mine!
With the plastic knobs all molten down and drooping
From leaving it on all the time,
And I know that's exactly what happens,
Because that's the way it happened to mine too,
And it's impossible to get the replacements,
And suddenly I smelt *my* Sunday stew, and *it* was burning!
I ran up the hall, and tripped, and took a terrible fall over the telephone cord,
And was lying on the floor, *with a broken arm*, can you *imagine?*
And I tried to call Gordon,
But the blasted cord had been pulled from the wall,
And you weren't there,
And I was alone.
And all I could hear was the flames and the Swedish,
And the woop, woop, woop of the fire alarm, and it was awful.
Graham, it was awful.

HUNTER: It's okay.

MARGARET: I'm just too old to be alone.

HUNTER: It's alright, Mum.

MARGARET: I just couldn't stay.

HUNTER: Nah. Of course not.
…
You couldn't stay there on your own,
Because instead of buying you a cordless phone
And maybe a new stove—

MARGARET: Stop it.

HUNTER: Or sending the girls around once a day,
Just to check on Grandma, make sure she's okay,
He went and drove you from your house.

MARGARET: That's enough out of you.
The pair of you!
You can't even try to get along.

HUNTER: I've heard some things.

MARGARET: Well, I don't care!
This'll do.
I don't complain.
It's probably more than I deserve.
I never should have said a word.
I should have kept my mouth shut.
I should have just sat here quietly.

HUNTER: No, Mum, I'm sorry. It's just …
It'll be alright. I don't know. Maybe I was just a bit jealous,
'Cause I thought that I'd be staying at the old place with you, ya know?
Mum? Just for a while. Just for a day or two,
I thought after all that time away,
We could spend some time together, working in the garden,
You know? Me and you, and, I dunno, maybe play …
Monopoly.

MARGARET: Oh, Graham.

HUNTER: I went past this afternoon.
You oughta see it.
Jacaranda trees, all startin' to bloom in the backyard.
Purple blossoms all startin' to grow.

MARGARET: The garden must look a mess.

HUNTER: Nothing that a bit of a mow wouldn't sort out.
That old Victa still in the shed?

MARGARET: Goodness me, I wouldn't know.

HUNTER: Or the old Land Rover?

MARGARET: You'd have to check with Gordon.

HUNTER: Wouldn't take much to get that old thing going again.

                      What you reckon, Mum?
                      Wanna come back and take a look at the old place too?

MARGARET: Oh, I don't know …

HUNTER: No?

MARGARET: Well … As a matter of fact, there might be a little thing
                      or two I left behind.
                      Just small things I couldn't quite find room for when I
                      packed.

HUNTER: Yeah? Anything of mine?

MARGARET: Well, a stack of model aeroplanes are under the stairs.
                      Your old schoolbooks. A football. A trophy … And there's
                      Your old air rifle, a blanket, and two teddy bears
                      Named Henry and Humphrey …

HUNTER: Alright, Mum.

MARGARET: And there's boxes and boxes of your old toy cars,
                      How you got that many, God only knows,
                      And then there's both of your little guitars,
                      From when you put on your musical shows …

HUNTER: Alright, Mum!

MARGARET: In the kitchen, there's pickles, and jams in jars,
                      And they should all still be perfectly fine.

HUNTER: Of course they would.

MARGARET: It's a waste to leave them, but when I was packing,
                      There just wasn't time.
                      And lots of old things that I'd like to sort through.

HUNTER: Of course you would, Mum. I understand.
                      It's settled then, I'll get the car running, I'll pick you up,
                      I'll give you a hand.
                      We can go for a walk in the garden together.

MARGARET: Maybe we could.

HUNTER: Why not? You and me?
                      Mum? … Mum, you know what else I'd like to see?
                      You remember all that land out back of the property?
                      Where me and Gordon used to go?

MARGARET: You used to have a name for it.

HUNTER: Do you remember?

MARGARET: You used to call it Etho.

HUNTER: Etho.

MARGARET: My goodness, so long ago,

HUNTER: We went there pretty much each day.

MARGARET: All that land, you boys could play
                       For hours, or the weekend, and you'd camp out there for
                       days.

HUNTER: Remember we made a fruit salad?

MARGARET: A fruit salad?

HUNTER: Of Etho fruits. Apples and oranges

MARGARET: And strawberries?

HUNTER: No strawberries.
                       Just fruits that used to grow around these rundown
                       orchards in Etho,
                       Oranges and apples, I think, and plums.

MARGARET: And you boys made a fruit salad.

HUNTER: These rundown fuckin' orchards, Mum.

MARGARET: Language.

HUNTER: Gordon found a grass snake.

MARGARET: Mulberries! Not strawberries.

HUNTER: Yeah, mulberries.

MARGARET: And chokos.

HUNTER: Yeah, but not in the fruit salad.

MARGARET: You boys come home with bags full,
                       Begging me to bake them into choko pies,
                       Or jams, or chutneys …

HUNTER: All tasted like shit.

MARGARET: Gordon found a grass snake?

HUNTER: In the orchard, and it bit him

MARGARET: No!

HUNTER: It did! It was sleeping and he poked it with a stick, the
                       stupid bugger.

MARGARET: And it bit him?

HUNTER: On the leg.

MARGARET: You never told me that.

HUNTER: I tied a tourniquet and put my shirt under his head

MARGARET: I think that I'd remember.

HUNTER: And then he turned all white.

MARGARET: I'm sure you never told me.

HUNTER: And I thought that he was dead.

MARGARET: No. You never told me that.

      …

      Was he alright?

      …

      Graham?

HUNTER: Huh?

MARGARET: Gordon, was he alright in the end?

HUNTER: No, Mum, he fucking died.

MARGARET: Graham!

HUNTER: So what do you reckon? The two of us! Tomorrow
      afternoon.
      We'll head out there together.

MARGARET: Does it need to be so soon, Graham?

HUNTER: Yes, Mum, yes! I'll clear a bit of room.
      I'll mow the lawn and fix the car
      And see if I can't come out here and get ya, Mum?
      The old place.
      The two of us we'll spend a while,
      Telling stories and sorting through pile after pile of
      leftover *shit!*
      Sorting through a dozen decades of pots and jams
      And porno magazines crammed under the crooked
      fuckin' floorboards,
      And teddy bears and toy cars
      And leftover memories, Mum,
      Of you, and me, and Gordon, and our dead father,
      And we'll wait, Mum, and we'll see
      If Gordon drives a bulldozer

Through a weatherboard wall,
And we hear the glass smash and the verandah crumple,
And the stumps that we lived and slept our childhoods on,
Coughed up like teeth and spat onto the ground.
And we'll see who he's been after all of this time!

MARGARET: Graham? Was Gordon alright in the end?

      …

HUNTER: Yeah, Mum … He was fine.

SCENE FOUR

HUNTER *and* GORDON *speak directly to the audience.*

GORDON: Hunter used to have this car—

HUNTER: It wasn't just a car.

GORDON: It was a *Land Rover.*

HUNTER: I had this fuckin' *Land Rover.*

GORDON: With a dodgy—

HUNTER: Everything. It had a dodgy everything.

GORDON: A steering thing, and yeah, yeah, pretty much everything!
And we were what? Seventeen?

HUNTER: *You* were.

GORDON: *You* woulda been …?

HUNTER: Fifteen or so, I dunno.

GORDON: So anyway! It had this dodgy steering thing. Whatcha
call it, Hunter?

HUNTER: Column.

GORDON: Had a dodgy steering column, didn't it?

HUNTER: You'd sit there and the whole thing would just lift off.

GORDON: In your hands! *In your hands!* It would just lift off!
So anyway—

HUNTER: So anyway—

GORDON: You go.

HUNTER: I was gonna say
The roads out near Talley are straight as—

GORDON: Straight as!

HUNTER: Straight as a gun barrel. The Old York Road, right?
            So anyway, this one time—
GORDON: You've got to say the hitchhiker.
HUNTER: I fucking am!
GORDON: We used to get these hitchhikers, going out to Talley. To
            see the Big Potato.
HUNTER: Like it's something to fuckin' see. So we'd stop—
GORDON: So we'd stop, right, Hunter would be driving.
HUNTER: Maybe smoking a joint or whatever.
GORDON: Well, *he* would be.
HUNTER: *I* would be. You'd be, maybe having a Fanta, or whatever?
GORDON: A beer or whatever, but anyway.
HUNTER: The hitchhiker's in the back, and offer him a bit of a
            smoke, and he'd be like,
            Nice one, thank you.
GORDON: He's off to Talley.
HUNTER: Off to see the Big Potato. And I'd be—
GORDON: Hunter's driving, and he'd be,
            'Do you feel like driving?' to me.
            And I'd be like—
HUNTER: Gordon's like, Nah.
GORDON: Nah.
HUNTER: 'Too tired' or whatever. So I turn to the hitchhiker—
GORDON: Gun barrel highway!
HUNTER: And say, 'What do you reckon? Do you want a go?'
GORDON: And he doesn't slow down …
HUNTER: And I pull out the steering wheel!
GORDON: Out of its column!
HUNTER: And pass it—
GORDON: He passes it—
HUNTER: Over my shoulder!
GORDON: And this guy's in the back, with a joint and a beer,
            And this one guy—
HUNTER: This German guy.

GORDON: He takes the wheel—
HUNTER: This German guy!
GORDON: He takes the wheel—
HUNTER: He takes the wheel!
GORDON & HUNTER: *And he starts to fuckin' steer!*

SCENE FIVE

Later the same day. It is the barbecue at Gordon and Rachel's house.

RACHEL, GORDON *and* HUNTER *come out of the house and onto the patio with drinks.*

HUNTER: They're absolutely lovely kids,
            They're really looking well.
GORDON: You see we did all this patio in a kind of caramel tile
            with a shell design.
RACHEL: Coralie plays a lot of sport.
            And Gracie likes reading books and things.
            Doesn't she, Gordon?
GORDON: With this kinda two-tone autumn variation here.
RACHEL: Gracie wants a pony,
            But there's not a lot of lawn.
GORDON: We've got six bedrooms here!
RACHEL: I don't know where we'd put it.
            The paddocks aren't that far, but she can't walk there on
            her own.
            She loves watching 'Pony Club' though, doesn't she
            Gordon,
            And she's got the tune on her mobile phone.

        GORDON *begins singing the 'Pony Club' theme.* HUNTER *speaks
        over him.*

HUNTER: Coralie plays …?
RACHEL: Basketball. At junior level.
            She's only in grade two.
GORDON: And netball!
RACHEL: Not netball.

GORDON: Yes!

RACHEL: No.

GORDON: What's the one with the net?

RACHEL: Volleyball. She plays mini-volleyball.

GORDON: And reads!
            Books!
            Christ, you oughta see her!
            Do you like Australian art?

RACHEL: Gordon's been collecting.

GORDON: Not Brett Whiteley, or Pro Hart,
            But I've got a few landscapes, yeah.
            You wanna take a look?

HUNTER: Actually, what I'd like to take's a shit.
            …

GORDON: Oh, that's charming. Thanks for sharing.

HUNTER: Thanks for caring.

            HUNTER *goes.*

GORDON: Jesus Christ. He hasn't changed a bit … Do you think?
            Rachel? … Do you think he's changed? He hasn't bloody
            changed a bit.

RACHEL: A little older.

GORDON: Maybe so. Aren't we all, but really though,
            I mean, really, you know?
            Really … I don't think he's bloody changed at all.

RACHEL: A little greyer.

GORDON: Aren't we all? Time goes by, the old snow starts to fall on
            the roof,
            But what I mean is more, this 'coming home', this 'poor
            old Mum',
            This 'look at me'! 'Prodigal son'. It's all so bloody
            typical.
            He doesn't write, he doesn't call for how long? Seven …

RACHEL: Seven and a half.

GORDON: … years?

He's filling Mum's head with these stupid ideas about the bloody house.

[*Quietly*] There's supposed be a settlement in a couple of—

RACHEL: The sale isn't for—

GORDON: Shhh!

RACHEL: I think I'm allowed to speak, Gordon.

GORDON: The girls shouldn't get attached.

RACHEL: Gordon.

GORDON: Just that—

RACHEL: He's their uncle.

GORDON: Just until, I don't know … just until we know. You know? What's going on.

RACHEL: We can't stand in his way.
             If he wants to read Gracie a story, or play a bit of basketball with Coralie.

GORDON: I suppose.

RACHEL: We've got nothing to hide. We've done nothing wrong.

GORDON: Of course not.

RACHEL: If he's—

GORDON: Of course not. Like what?

RACHEL: If he's … Let's just enjoy the night,
             And get along, and be polite,
             And who knows whether he'll even be here tomorrow.

HUNTER: Oh, I reckon that I might.

    HUNTER *has returned.*

GORDON: That was quick.

HUNTER: Went away. Just like that.
             Stopped in to say goodnight to the girls instead.

    Silence.

GORDON: Well, it must be almost time to eat.

RACHEL: Are you hungry, Hunter?

HUNTER: Starving.

GORDON: Well, I might just go …
            I might just go and check the meat.

            GORDON *goes. Silence.*

HUNTER: So. This is strange.

RACHEL: You think?

HUNTER: Well, the last time us two—

RACHEL: We saw each other this afternoon.

HUNTER: We did. Yeah. We did, that's true.
            But before that …

RACHEL: Before that was a very long time ago.
            You've been off gallivanting,
            Must be quite nice being you.

HUNTER: You've got no idea.

RACHEL: Well, I've got no idea what you're doing here.

HUNTER: You invited me.

RACHEL: To a barbecue.
            I wanted you to meet the girls, and feel like you're part
            of a family.
            But, Hunter, it's important that we both know where we
            stand.

HUNTER: Which is?

RACHEL: I don't know what you think you might have come back
            here to find,
            But if it's anything more than being an uncle to your
            nieces,
            And helping with your mother, and adding to a happy
            home.

HUNTER: What more could I want?

RACHEL: There are no missing pieces here. And we've all grown
            A great deal since you've been away.
            At least I have.
            Have you?

HUNTER: You tell me.
            …

RACHEL:	And here I was convinced
	You'd have a family of your own.
	Gordon said you wouldn't but always I hoped you would.
	No wife, Hunter?
HUNTER:	Not for me.
RACHEL:	No children?
HUNTER:	Nah.
RACHEL:	No reason why you disappeared?
	No love stories to tell? No found-true-love-upon-the-road?
	No broken hearts or broken homes?
	You always fell in love so fast.
HUNTER:	I did, that's true.
RACHEL:	No darling to adore you? The way you like to be adored?
	To have them fall in love with you,
	I find that hard to understand.
HUNTER:	Actually, it isn't.
RACHEL:	I suppose that people change.
HUNTER:	After spending time in prison
	Rachel, I suppose they do.
	…
RACHEL:	You were on the rigs.
HUNTER:	Maybe I lied.
	Maybe I broke a heart or two inside, I couldn't say.
	Kids though? Nah. Not in there.
	Not enough, you know, open air, for them to run around and play.
	My God, your kids are looking well.
RACHEL:	Hunter, why would you tell me that?
	I don't even believe you.
HUNTER:	I told you I'd come back.
RACHEL:	Not after seven years!
	…
	[*Quietly*] This is me. Here. See?
	This is me now.

	I make my girls sandwiches. I wash their hair,

I make my girls sandwiches. I wash their hair,
I take them to the swimming pool.
We don't eat tuna because Coralie loves the dolphins.
Gordon's a good husband and I'm a good wife.

HUNTER: Right.

RACHEL: When he says he'll be somewhere, he'll be somewhere.
He takes the girls to school and he remembers my
birthday.
And he takes out the big bins on Saturday nights.

HUNTER: Does he know?

RACHEL: Know what?
There's nothing to know.
If you want, you can go right now.
It doesn't all revolve around you, you know.
And if we had some sort of stupid thoughts
Seven years ago,
What happened then, stays back then and stays between
us two.

…

Do you understand? Hunter?

GORDON *has entered.*

GORDON: So we bought this bloody *barbecue*
On Visa card credit points!
Didn't we, sweetheart?
We bought enough … stuff.
Just … stuff on Visa over the years.
Collected a hundred and fifty thousand fuckin' points.
Imagine that!
And bought this … grill cooker.
This big, fuck-you … grill and bloody barbecue,
And the meat's as sweet … wait till we eat …
Can you check on the girls, love,
I want to show Hunter some of this art.

RACHEL: Maybe in a moment.

GORDON: Could you do it now please, sweetheart?

Coralie said she couldn't sleep and really wants to speak with you.

RACHEL *goes.*

Do you like the wine, Hunter?
Vintner's Blend. It's from the Barossa.

HUNTER *drinks his beer.*

Let's get down to business then, will we?
I suppose you've noticed—

HUNTER: What a total fuckin' tosser you've become?
Yeah, I've noticed.

GORDON: I hear you stopped to visit Mum ggain this afternoon.

HUNTER: I'm gonna help her move back home.

GORDON: You're not.

HUNTER: Afraid I am. She practically begged me to.

GORDON: It's not gonna happen.

HUNTER: I'm—

GORDON: You tell her all this crap an'
I'm the one who has to deal with it after you go.

HUNTER: I'm gonna need a key.

GORDON: Okay, let's get one thing clear.
You're not gonna move Mum back there on her own,
In an empty house, in the middle of a construction zone.
It's ridiculous.

HUNTER: There's other people wanna stay.

GORDON: There's no-one.

HUNTER: Not everybody wants to sell.

GORDON: There's no—tell me one person who—

HUNTER: There's others! Other people. Being pushed outta their home,
Like you're pushing Mum.

GORDON: Even if she wanted to stay, which she doesn't,
It wouldn't change the fact that there are four beneficiaries,
You, me, Coralie and Gracie.

And three of us reckon the place is too old
And it's falling down around her and it's ready to be sold,
And even if you got Mum onside with you,
It'd make no difference 'cause it's three against two.
Okay?
But listen—

HUNTER: So it's all about the numbers, is it?

GORDON: Listen—yes it is—but listen, I care about you.
And you're my brother,
And I'm concerned for your wellbeing too,
And I realise that it might not be that easy coming home.
And I appreciate this business with the house
Might have thrown you a little.
And I understand.
And if it makes things any easier, until the sale goes through,
I thought, maybe I could lend you a helping hand.
If you know what I mean?
…
Just think about it.
Now, I wanted to show you some of this art.

HUNTER: How much am I supposed to be thinking?

GORDON: It's just a small collection.

HUNTER: How much?

GORDON: We're just standing here drinking, Hunter.

HUNTER: Just give me a figure.

GORDON: Australian artists mostly.
Landscapes.

HUNTER: You'd pay to see me go?

GORDON: I said no such thing.

HUNTER: Actually, you know what this one reminds me of?
Kinda reminds me of Etho.
Remember how the branches used to come out from the dam?
We used to call 'em dead man's hands, remember?

Like someone underwater reaching up into the air.
Just reaching out for something, but of course, there's
nothing there,
Is there, Gordon?

GORDON: Anyway, Hunter, if there's anything I can do.

HUNTER: How about half a million dollars?

...

GORDON: Oh, you know what, *fuck you too.*

HUNTER: You're the one who brought it up, mate, you asked my
price.

GORDON: I asked you as my brother if you were in trouble, Hunter,
Jesus Christ!

HUNTER: Five hundred thousand dollars, and I'll leave right now.

GORDON: Actually, Hunter, it might be time for you to go.

HUNTER: Give me the keys to the old house.

GORDON: I'm giving you nothing.
There's a sale coming up, and Mum's moved out.

HUNTER: But she isn't fucking dead,
However much you wish she was!
And she can move back anytime she wants.

GORDON: Yeah? Check your facts.

HUNTER: It still belongs to her!

GORDON: And you're an expert on inheritance tax now, are you?
She signed everything over to a sole trustee,
And, obviously, as the girls' father, that was going to be
me. Alright?

HUNTER: I want the keys to the house.

GORDON: Let it go, Hunter.

HUNTER: You're gonna give me the keys.

GORDON: You know what, just go.
Get out of my sight!

RACHEL: Hunter, what have you said to Coralie?

RACHEL *has entered.*

HUNTER: Nothing.

GORDON: What? Is she alright?

RACHEL: She can't sleep.

HUNTER: If she can't sleep, she can't sleep.

GORDON: What the fuck? What did you say?

HUNTER: Nothing.

RACHEL: Hunter.

HUNTER: I just asked her about basketball,
           And said we might play a game together on the weekend.

GORDON: Is she alright?

RACHEL: I think you should go.

HUNTER: I told her I used to play basketball too, as a kid.
           And then she asked me about you, Gordon,
           And I said no, I don't think you ever actually did.
           Did you?

RACHEL: Get out.

HUNTER: How old is she now? Almost seven?
           The only thing I said—

GORDON: Get out of here.

HUNTER: —And you know, this is true,
           Is that she almost looks as much like me as she looks like
           you,
           That's all I said.

GORDON: Get the fuck out of my house or I'll call the police.

RACHEL: How dare you!

HUNTER: Family, huh?

GORDON: Get out of here, Hunter, or I won't be responsible for
           my—

HUNTER: *Thanks for the wine!*
           But if there's even the slightest possible chance that
           she's mine,
           Then with Mum on my side, that's three against two,
           So let's say for the moment, there's no sale going through.
           You got that?
           I'm stayin' at the pub. You can drop off the keys.

HUNTER *goes.*

RACHEL *looks at* GORDON.

RACHEL: Oh, for God's sake, Gordon.
            Gordon, please!
            Don't be so bloody childish, you know it's not true!

GORDON *goes.*

            Gordon!

END OF ACT ONE

ACT TWO

GORDON *and* WALKER. *The girls are imagined into the scene and do
not appear.*

GORDON: Say, 'Ah'.
    …
    Say, 'Ah', that's it.
    Ahhh.
    …
    That's my girl.
    …
    That's Daddy's good girl.
    Are you Daddy's good girl?
    …
    Sergeant.

WALKER: I, Sergeant Alfred Walker,
    Witness that upon this day
    A saliva swab was taken in my presence
    From the mouth of one Grace Anne Smeaton

GORDON: Daddy's good girl

WALKER: A person who is known to me
    And known to be five years of age.

GORDON: Have a Kinder Surprise.

WALKER: And I declare I witness that the
    Aforementioned swab was placed
    In my presence and sealed
    In specimen container marked D3CA119—

GORDON: It's a mermaid.

WALKER: —210.

GORDON: A fish.
    Ariel? No?
    Pokémon? No?

	Pocahontas? No?
	Nemo!
WALKER:	Sealed saliva sample D3CA119-210.
GORDON:	Daddy's special girl.

Pause as Gracie goes off and Coralie arrives.

	Say, 'Ah'.
	…
	Say, 'Ah', sweetheart.
	Cup of tea, sergeant?
WALKER:	Nah, thanks, nah,
GORDON:	Say, 'Ah'.
	Kinder Surprise?
	No Kinder Surprise.
	Open.
WALKER:	How about a hair?
GORDON:	What?
WALKER:	You can use a hair.
	Sometimes you can use a hair if the suspect is recalcitrant.
GORDON:	She's not—Say, 'Ah'.
	…
	Coralie, say, 'Ah'.
	Show Daddy how you—say 'Ah'.
	Coralie!
	…
	Are you Daddy's good girl?
	…
	Are you Daddy's girl?
	Are you?
	…
	Sorry, sergeant, this won't take a minute.
	Say, 'Ahhh'?
	…
	Good girl!
WALKER:	I, Sergeant Alfred Walker—
	Now my fuckin' pen's not working.
GORDON:	Sergeant!

WALKER: Sorry. I, Sergeant Alfred Walker …

GORDON: What's this? A platypus?
            A tractor?
            You have to put the bits together.

WALKER: Fuckin' hell.
            Can I use this?

GORDON: You have to put the bits together!

WALKER: Wiggles. It's a Wiggles pen.

GORDON: Like this.
            No, like this.

WALKER: Witness that upon this day
            A saliva swab was taken in my presence
            From the mouth of one Coralie Smeaton,
            A person who is known to me
            And known to be *seven?*

GORDON: Seven.

WALKER: *Seven* years of age.

GORDON: Don't you want your chocolate, sweetheart?

WALKER: And I declare I witness that—

GORDON: Coralie?

WALKER: —the
            Aforementioned swab was placed
            In my presence and sealed
            In specimen container D3CA119-288.
            All done.

GORDON: Good girl.

WALKER: All clear.

GORDON: Good girl.
            …

WALKER: Any chance of a beer?

SCENE TWO

A twenty-dollar room above a pub. HUNTER *has opened the door to a
furious* RACHEL.

RACHEL: *You couldn't help yourself, could you?!*

HUNTER: I—

RACHEL: *You had to pick at it to see if you could make it bleed!*

HUNTER: I just—

RACHEL: *A schoolboy with a scabby knee!*
You had to pick and pick at it, to squeeze
Out that last bit of pus!

HUNTER: I'll tell him!

RACHEL: *Squeeze out that last bit of—*
What? You'll tell him what?
That his wife's not a whore?
That's very helpful, Hunter, thank you!

HUNTER: That what happened between you and me was before …
…
I'm sorry.

RACHEL: Yes, I bet you are!

HUNTER: I'll explain.

RACHEL: Oh, it's gone too far for that I'm afraid!
Gordon's gone stupid with mouth-swabs and rubber gloves,
He'd DNA the dog if he could!

HUNTER: There's no need.

RACHEL: Who are you telling, Hunter? *Me?*
I know there's no need!

HUNTER: I'm sorry!

RACHEL: *You're* the one who turned me into nothing
But a cheap bloody booby prize between you two,
I swear that I could murder you,
And you can go straight to hell as far as I'm concerned,
Although you'd think I would have learned by now,
When you and your brother
Get busy getting off on getting even with each other,
That feelings of respect, heaven forbid, *respect?*
Go out the bloody window.

Kill each other then! I don't care anymore!
As long as you leave *my* children
Out of your juvenile, dick-comparing war,
I don't care what you do,
Do you understand me, Hunter?!

Silence.

How could you?

HUNTER: I don't want him to sell the land.

RACHEL: *I think we've got that part of it, Hunter.*
I think we *understand* that bit.

HUNTER: I'm sorry.

            …

Rachel? I'm really sorry.

            …

I've missed you—

RACHEL: Oh. Just. Don't.

HUNTER: Does he know you're here?

Silence.

RACHEL: This place stinks.

HUNTER: You can't open the—

RACHEL: I'm no expert but I doubt that sink's supposed to have
socks in it.

HUNTER: I'm doing my washing and the window's stuck.

RACHEL: Well, get another room.

HUNTER: I was lucky to get this one.
There's no call for accommodation here anymore.
At least with this one you can lock the door.
And it's got a sink.

RACHEL: To wash your socks.

HUNTER: And the toilet's broken up the hall.

RACHEL: Oh … Ew.

Silence.

What are you doing here, Hunter?

HUNTER:	I don't want him to sell.
RACHEL:	Apart from that.
	I mean what are you actually doing here?
HUNTER:	I don't know. Catching up.
RACHEL:	Really? Catching up with?
HUNTER:	Family. Friends.
RACHEL:	Friends?
HUNTER:	Strangers.
	Catching up with the news, catching up with the changes.

Pause.

	They built a fountain.
RACHEL:	It was a Community Development Project.
HUNTER:	It looks like shit.
RACHEL:	They didn't quite finish.
HUNTER:	It looks ridiculous.
RACHEL:	It'll look better when they put water into it.
HUNTER:	It's all just *changed*. It's all just … gone.
RACHEL:	Of course it's changed.
HUNTER:	The butcher and the pie shop and the milk bar.
RACHEL:	There's a new supermarket and a new hairdressing salon
	In case you hadn't noticed.
HUNTER:	Who needs that shit?
RACHEL:	Not you obviously.
HUNTER:	It's all just wrong.
RACHEL:	Things change.
HUNTER:	It's all just …
	…
	They closed the old bank
RACHEL:	Yes, they did,
HUNTER:	They closed the bank and they opened a cafe.
RACHEL:	Yes.
HUNTER:	And called it *The Bank?!*
RACHEL:	Yes.

HUNTER: So what, now you have to go a hundred k to Talley
            To get to your money,
            But for a *frappe-fuckin'-chino* and a *Thai chicken salad?*

RACHEL: There's an ATM at the IGA.

HUNTER: But there's—

RACHEL: And we can't all live on pies and chocolate milk.
            …
            Things change, Hunter. It's been a long time.

HUNTER: No. It's not just that. It's …
            Have you been to the bar downstairs? It's a fuckin' joke.
            Nothing but poker machines and pissheads
            And kids who are drinking bourbon and Coke as if it's a
            real fuckin' drink,
            It's ridiculous!

RACHEL: Then go.

HUNTER: I can't.
            …
            It's like I'm the only one who knows how it's s'posed to
            be.

RACHEL: Oh, Hunter … listen to yourself.

HUNTER: No, seriously. It's like I'm the only one who can see
            What the fuck is going on.

RACHEL: And what the fuck *is* going on?

HUNTER: It's *changing*.

RACHEL: Yes!

HUNTER: No! I know, but we need to get it back.

RACHEL: Get what back?
            What?
            The past? What?
            Our twenties? What?

HUNTER: I just—

RACHEL: The pie shop?
            It's gone, Hunter! It's over!
            It isn't coming back.

HUNTER: But it's not how it's supposed to be.

RACHEL: I understand that seeing it all suddenly,
It's like a shock. But it all happens over time.
It all happens piece by piece.
The old butcher hits retirement,
There's no-one left to take the lease,
Things end.
Things change.
I've missed you too but can't you see
There comes a time when people like you and me,
We just have to let it go.
We're not in charge of it anymore, Hunter.
Look at us.
It doesn't belong to *us* anymore.

HUNTER: Who does it belong to?

RACHEL: I don't know.
Coralie? Gracie?

HUNTER: No.

RACHEL: The next generation?

HUNTER: No! Don't you see?
That's the point! It doesn't belong to them at all!
That's the exact point. It *doesn't* belong to them.
It belongs to a bunch of bankers! It belongs to investors.
It belongs to developers and, excuse me, but those fucking wankers
And their friendly fucking building societies.
Ask yourself, Rachel. No. Ask yourself why it is
That they suddenly want all this property?
So that they can make more money for themselves,
Out of more people, for themselves,
With our land! For themselves! And we're letting them.
They're *stealing* it from the next generation!
They're *stealing* it from Coralie and Gracie!
And what are they building in return?
Basically just slums.
More and more slums.
A thousand houses stacked together

Sniffing up each other's bums.
With no room for nothing!
For trees to climb,
Or bush or snakes or shortcuts
Or tracks to smash your bike along.
They're taking it, Rachel,
Everything we grew up on!
And I'm not going to let them!

RACHEL: Hunter, it's already gone.

            …

            I'm sorry. But it's already gone.

            …

            Open your eyes.
            Have you had a proper look around?
            It's all surveyed and subdivided.
            They've marked out the lots and the blocks and decided
            Which stages to release when.
            It's all already happening.

HUNTER: We can—

RACHEL: No we can't!
            They'll build right up to your boundary!
            Up to the edge of your land and surround every—

HUNTER: But if—

RACHEL: They'll push and they'll squeeze,
            And then when you've lost the last possible reason
            To stay …
            That's when they'll turn around and they'll pay
            You a quarter, an eighth, of what they're offering now.

HUNTER: But if we all stick together—

RACHEL: *Who?*

HUNTER: There's people holding out.

RACHEL: *There's not.*

HUNTER: There's people who don't want to sell.

RACHEL: *They've sold.*
            The last of them.
            A few tried to hold out but everybody folded in the end.

A few of us get to stay in the area.
The girls finish primary school where their teacher
knows their name.
…
We got to support the corner shop
Until the supermarket came,
But that's the best we can hope for.
That's the best we can do.
…
This old room will be the last thing left.
…
With its bedspread
…
And black-and-white television.

HUNTER: That doesn't work.

RACHEL: That doesn't work.
…
And kettle … And you.
…
I'm sorry but it's just time to let it go.
…
Hunter?
I'm sorry.

HUNTER: [*surrendering*] Dad left that property to his children and
his grandchildren.

RACHEL: Then let it be worth something.
Let it be worth leaving to someone.
Talk to your brother and work out together how the sale
can go through.
It's the best thing for everyone at this stage, Hunter,
For your nieces, for us.
It's the best thing for you.
I'm sure you can use the money,
Help you make a fresh start.
God knows we can.

HUNTER: Don't tell me Australian art hasn't made Gordon a
millionaire.

RACHEL: Don't even get me going on that.
            Coralie starts at St Agnes next year,
            And then there's the payments on your mother's flat,
            Please don't think we're flush.

HUNTER: You should have stuck with me.

RACHEL: And don't even make jokes about that either.

HUNTER: Just saying. Maybe you could have done a bit better.

RACHEL: Right. All this and more?

HUNTER: Yeah.

RACHEL: A twenty-dollar hotel room.

HUNTER: With a lockable front door, don't forget that.

RACHEL: After seven years without a letter.

HUNTER: Well, maybe you could have been with me.

RACHEL: In prison?

HUNTER: That was only a couple of weeks … I got locked into a
            bottle shop.
                …

RACHEL: I think I made the right decision.

HUNTER: Just saying that—

RACHEL: I'm happy.

HUNTER: Are you, Rache?

RACHEL: I love my husband.

HUNTER: Really?

RACHEL: I'm telling you that I do.

HUNTER: And you trust each other?

RACHEL: Yes.

HUNTER: Then why's he making you sit through
            A DNA test?

RACHEL: *Whose fault is that?!*

HUNTER: But he shouldn't be, should he?
                …
            Should he?

RACHEL: He's a good man. That's all that matters.
            All the rest just fades away.

HUNTER:	Right. And just so long as he can pay For that fuckin' fortress that you live in.
RACHEL:	You're not even listening to me!
HUNTER:	Just so long as he keeps coughing up For more caramel design exterior decorating.
RACHEL:	This is not about money!
HUNTER:	No?
RACHEL:	We're in debt up to our ears! For your information, we'd be paying off our mortgage For another hundred years If this sale didn't go through. But I'm happy. With him. With Gordon. For who he is. Do you understand? I love *him*.

Silence.

HUNTER:	Another hundred years?
RACHEL:	It's an expression.
HUNTER:	So you don't own your house?
RACHEL:	We're paying it off.
HUNTER:	So you took out a loan?
RACHEL:	And we're paying it—
HUNTER:	Because you suddenly had some security?
RACHEL:	What?
HUNTER:	Because suddenly the old house was worth something.
RACHEL:	What? We took out a loan Because that's what people do.
HUNTER:	*On the strength of a property* *That didn't even belong to you.* That's what I'm asking.
RACHEL:	No.
HUNTER:	Yes. When you bought your new house you must have known That they were developing the old place, To secure that kind of loan? Is that right?

RACHEL: We knew there was interest. Everybody knew.

HUNTER: So you kicked out Mum and you met with the banks /

RACHEL: Don't be so—

HUNTER: And next thing you know, it's thanks very much
            Here's a loan for a million dollars.
            Is that what happened?

RACHEL: Don't be so—

HUNTER: *I should have known!*

RACHEL: *You* don't know anything!

HUNTER: I should have fucking known!
            You weren't the last ones to hold out!
            You were the first two people on the phone
            To find a fuckin' buyer!

RACHEL: That's nonsense!

HUNTER: Is it? Tell me to my face,
            That you hadn't already decided on the new place
            When you moved Mum out.
            …

RACHEL: I can't remember.

HUNTER: Does Gordon know you're here?
            …
            Does he?

RACHEL: *Yes!* But only because—

HUNTER: Tell him—

RACHEL: Only because I told him I was—

HUNTER: Tell him—

RACHEL: Just let me say—

HUNTER: It's gonna take a lot more than a bit of DNA
            For me to let go of that land!

RACHEL: It's not / *yours to let go of.*

HUNTER: / Dad left the property to his *children* and his
                     grandchildren,
            And that includes me!
            I'm moving Mum back in.

> I'm stopping the sale.
> He can bring in the trucks
> But I promise you, they'll
> Have to Run. Us. Fucking. Over.

RACHEL: *Hunter!* … We could lose our house.

HUNTER: No, Rachel! We could save it!

> …

RACHEL: There's no talking to you, is there?

HUNTER: Tell him that!

   RACHEL *goes.*

> Tell him Mum's moving out of that flat,
> Back into the house where she's supposed to be.
> Tell him, I'm gonna put everything back,
> I'll make everything right. You can tell him from me!
> Rachel?
> If he wants a fight? He'll get one.
> You'll see.
> [*Calling out behind her*] The whole fuckin' lot of you!
> Just you wait and see!

SCENE THREE

HUNTER *and* GORDON *speak directly to the audience.*

GORDON: Great-grandad Ken only had one arm
           And his brother only had one eye.

HUNTER: And together they built the house we grew up in
           And we always reckoned that that was the reason
           Everything's crooked as shit.

GORDON: It'd look okay if you were standing out the front of it.

HUNTER: You'd roll out of bed and you wouldn't know why.

GORDON: And the pile of buttered bread used to tilt
           And then slide right off the dining room table.

HUNTER: Things used to slide around a fair bit,
           But apart from that—

GORDON: it was all quite stable.

HUNTER: Well …
GORDON: Well … kinda.
        …
HUNTER: They built the house on a block of land
That Ken had picked up over a hand of poker
With a strapper
Who was found drowned two days later.
Everyone said it was cursed.
Great-grandad Ken got married.
GORDON: And his brother took to drinking.
HUNTER: Although no-one was surprised when old great-grandad
Ken died first.
His brother lived to be about a hundred.
GORDON: Ken left the place to his five children and his
grandchildren
And died before he learned
That all five boys went to war
But only one of them returned.
The youngest. William.
Who everyone called Pony.
HUNTER: The other four are written on the Forges side of the war
memorial:
        Smeaton, Cecil.
        Smeaton, Charles.
        Smeaton, Harry.
        Smeaton, James.
Only Pony came back.
He was twenty-one.
GORDON: And his mum went mad with a broken heart,
She'd sit there with a loaded gun
And shoot at any bloody kids that came anywhere near
her.
She had to be put away.
HUNTER: William stayed long enough
To marry his childhood sweetheart,
A schoolteacher's daughter by name of Maureen.
They had a kid together until he went out for cigarettes.

GORDON: That was the joke,
Went out for cigarettes and didn't even smoke.

HUNTER: And they reckon that's the last time that he was ever seen.

GORDON: Leaving Maureen and baby Graham.

HUNTER: Our dad.

GORDON: Strangers in a strange house,
Stuck there on their own.

HUNTER: And she just started eatin'
Couldn't stop herself.

GORDON: Pack of biscuits'd no sooner come down off the pantry
shelf
Than she'd be shovelling 'em down her gob.

HUNTER: Dad had to be taken away—

GORDON: To an uncle in Merimbula or an aunty out in Hay.
They sent him home again when he was about nine.

HUNTER: And old Gramma Smeaton, mate's, been eatin' this entire
time.

GORDON: She was fuckin' huge!

HUNTER: She had to get these special dresses made from the
maternity store!

GORDON: And in my room you could still make out
These two dents on the hardwood floor
From where she landed her fat feet when she got out of
bed in the morning.
They put her in the ground, it took half the town to carry
her
And Dad had a buggered shoulder from that day till his
last.
…
And Dad was just Dad.

HUNTER: When *he* died, the pub flew its flag at half mast.

GORDON: He was a good man.

HUNTER: He was a prick.

GORDON: As if you'd know.

HUNTER: Of course I would.

GORDON: As if you wouldn't pack up and go
            Every time that he so much as coughed.

    Pause.

HUNTER: Dad left the place to *his* children and *his* grandchildren.
            A house for them to live
            Just a couple of acres,
            That's all he had to give,
            That's all he left behind.
            Because frankly, he was a cheap bastard
            Who'd suck the dry end of a stick if he thought there was
            a drink in it for him.

MARGARET: [*from off*] Graham!

HUNTER: *And raised a fist to you too, Mum, if the truth be told!*
            But all that I'm sayin',
            And you know this is true.
            All I'm sayin' …
            …
            Is that Dad never sold.
            Even Dad never sold.

SCENE FOUR

The police station.

SERGEANT WALKER *is packing up. Boxes are on the floor and on the table. He has a trophy in his hand as* HUNTER *enters.*

WALKER: Hunter!

HUNTER: [*looking around*] What's goin' on here?

WALKER: Look at this!

HUNTER: What's goin' on here?

WALKER: World's Best Coach. See? Under sixteens.

    He passes the trophy to HUNTER.

HUNTER: If you were the world's best coach
            How come none of our teams
            Ever made the top four?

WALKER: Bad luck I suppose.

HUNTER: There were five clubs in the comp.

WALKER: Six.

HUNTER: Lawler kids were retards.

WALKER: Mate!

HUNTER: 'Special school' retards or whatever.

WALKER: They were big though.

HUNTER: They were huge, but they couldn't kick a ball.
They used to hit themselves in the face.

WALKER: That only happened once.

HUNTER: Whenever Big Josh got the footy
He ran all the way back to his place
And locked himself in the garage.

WALKER: They beat us one year though.

HUNTER: Yeah they did … Yeah, they did I know …
World's Best Coach.

He hands it back.

              That's what you wanted to see me about, was it?

WALKER: No, mate, no.
I have some official duties to … officiate,
And as you know
Your brother's asked me to look after this blood test caper.

HUNTER: I gave you a sample a couple of days ago!

WALKER: Yes, mate, yes.
They've come back. The tests.
The results. I got 'em here.

HUNTER: Well, it's all just a waste of time.
…
I never actually said that the kid was mine,
I said … All I said was …
I've apologised to Rachel.

WALKER: She's a good—

HUNTER: I know she is.
But I'm not giving up the property.

WALKER: Maybe you should just think about—

HUNTER: I am not giving up the property!
            Me and Mum are gonna move back in.
            There's some good people wanna stay …

        HUNTER *looks around.*

            Hold on. You wanna tell me what's goin' on here, Alf?
WALKER: Nothin'.
            …
            Just doin' a bit of cleaning.
            I told ya they were closing this place down.
HUNTER: Not yet though.
WALKER: No, not yet.
            Actually, I'm retiring.
HUNTER: Retiring?
WALKER: Yeah.
HUNTER: When?
WALKER: Soon … Pretty soon … Now.
            Got a replacement coming down from Talley.
HUNTER: What?
WALKER: Just seems right somehow.
            You know?
            You know when it's time to go,
            You know?
            I got long service leave comin' out my arse.
            …
HUNTER: Where you off to?
WALKER: [*with a shrug*] Gold Coast.
            … What?
            I like a bit of sun as much as the next man.
            Drink a bit of beer, get myself a suntan.
HUNTER: Is that so?
WALKER: Little apartment, directly on the water,
            It's a buyer's market they reckon,
            Mate, you oughta—
HUNTER: [*suddenly angry*] I oughta what?!

WALKER: You know what they say …
            Opportunity knocks …

HUNTER: Hmm?

WALKER: Opportunity knocks, open the fuckin' door or something,
            I don't know.
            …

HUNTER: It was you, wasn't it?
            You were the only one still tryin' to hold on to some
            land.

WALKER: I only had a couple of acres.

HUNTER: Fuck me!

WALKER: There's a line, Hunter. Between principles and stupidity,
            And it woulda been plain bloody stupid for me
            To hold out any longer.
            Stupid to keep saying no.
            I'm fifty-eight years old.
            I got two years left to go,
            And then what? Eh?
            …
            It hasn't been easy, mate.
            But what else could I do?
            The amount of memories in this station …

        GORDON *enters.*

            We were just talking about you!

GORDON: Let's get on with it.

        Silence. GORDON *and* HUNTER *glare at each other.*

WALKER: Can't shake hands, lads?

GORDON: Let's get on with it!

WALKER: Surely the two of you—

GORDON: *Just get on with it!*
            …

HUNTER: I've already said that there isn't any need.

GORDON: You're the one who started it.

HUNTER: And then I agreed

	To drop any claim. Gordon, I never even said that she was mine
	You just bloody jumped to a conclusion.
GORDON:	Well, let's all avoid any possible confusion in the future, Hunter,
	And get this out of the way.
HUNTER:	It'll make no difference.
GORDON:	*To me it fucking will!*
WALKER:	Alright now, boys.
	…
GORDON:	Okay. So the one undisputed thing is that according to Dad's will—
HUNTER:	He left the place—
GORDON:	To his children and his grandchildren.
	So let's just establish that *his* grandchildren are *mine*,
	Let's just establish that there's a clear, direct, undisputed line
	Between him and them. I think that's for the best.
HUNTER:	I'm not going to let you—
GORDON:	And once that's done, Hunter,
	Once that's established,
	We'll let the courts decide the rest.
	That's all I've got to say.
HUNTER:	I'm not going to—
GORDON:	That's all I've got to say!
	Sergeant?
WALKER:	Right.
GORDON:	Oh, and I'd get myself a lawyer by the way.
	Sergeant?

WALKER *opens the envelope.*

WALKER:	I, Sergeant Alfred Walker, witness that upon this—
GORDON:	Just get on with it.
	…
WALKER:	[*clearing his throat and reading*] 'Thank you for receipt of the fee.

     …
     Sixteen genetic loci were tested
     Including AMEL, TH01, TPOX, Penta E …'

HUNTER: / Just get the fuck … /

GORDON: / Just get the fuck on with it!

WALKER: Alright, alright …
     'Based on DNA analysis, the alleged father *Gordon*
     Smeaton
     Cannot be excluded as the biological father of the child
     Coralie Smeaton
     Sharing significant genetic markers in the samples
     provided and sent,
     With a probability percentage of paternity estimated
     At around 99.9942 percent.
     Conversely, based on the DNA analysis, the alleged
     father *Graham* Smeaton
     Is excluded as the biological father of the child
     With shared genetic markers being insignificantly low,
     And a probability percentage of paternity estimated at
     zero.'

HUNTER: You happy?

GORDON: And Gracie?

WALKER: [*reading*] Zero as well.

GORDON: My lawyers will be in touch after the sale.
     Thank you, sergeant.

HUNTER: I won't let you—

GORDON: No? And what do you plan to do?
     You've got nothing, Hunter.
     You've got no leg to stand on.

HUNTER: I—

GORDON: They're my children, my wife,
     My house, my life!
     You have got nothing, Hunter. There's just you!
     …
     You'll get what you're entitled to *by law*

After the sale's gone through.
Now excuse me—

WALKER: There's more.

…

It says, 'Disputes between brothers are rarely conclusive
As all siblings share identical Y STR.
It is only because these samples have been taken from
half-brothers,
That the findings returned are as unambiguous as they
are.'

…

GORDON: What?

HUNTER: What?

…

WALKER: 'These brothers do not share a common paternal stem.'

HUNTER: That's bullshit.

GORDON: That's bullshit. Of course we fuckin' do.

WALKER: A relational index of point zero, zero, two
           Suggests otherwise.

HUNTER: How could I not have the same father as him?

…

WALKER: Well …

HUNTER: I don't mean *how*, I mean …

WALKER: Strewth!

Silence.

HUNTER: Did you know?

WALKER: Me? No! God no.
           Mind you, neither of ya looks that much like Graham
           Senior to tell you the truth.

GORDON: What's *that* supposed to mean?!

WALKER: Nothing! Nothing. Jesus. Just … nothing.

Silence.

Who wants a beer?

GORDON: Okay. Dad left the land to *his* children and *his* grandchildren,
            And, Hunter, *if this is true*,
            You can be Little Orphan Annie for all I fuckin' care,
            But you will get nothing from me.

HUNTER: What makes ya think it's you?

GORDON: Huh?

HUNTER: What makes you think it's you?

    Silence.

WALKER: Fuck, I could do with a beer.

    GORDON *turns and goes.*

HUNTER: Gordon!
            Gordon, come back, ya nong. It'll be a mistake!

    GORDON *is gone.*

            It'll be a mistake.

WALKER: Bound to be.
            …
            You feel like a beer, mate?
            Sit down. Let's have a beer.
            Mind you, it's not the strangest thing ever to happen around here,
            Not by a long shot.

He goes out back to get beer.

            I could tell you a thing or two …
            Actually, Hunter, you know what?
            Look what I found,
            Forty-year-old scotch!
            I scored a dozen off that fella Licensing asked me to watch
            Before they raided him one arvo.
            The whole operation was botched
            Because Ballarat Police were playing Talley in the quarters
            And the whole town was overrun by busloads of police.

    HUNTER *leaves.*

By the time of the raid I mean, this guy had bolted,
By the time of the raid, Christ he musta been at least
Halfway to Darwin, I reckon.

WALKER *returns. He stands in his empty police station with the
scotch bottle and two glasses.*

Hunter?
…
Not always easy to return stolen goods.
…
Hunter?
…

*He pours himself a glass. The lights slowly go down as he
makes his way around the station.*

God, this place though, it's like there's memories
everywhere.
Little Jillie Harrington was born right on that fuckin'
chair,
Her mother screaming murder there was blood and
women's underwear,
Her old man in the lockup
For two thousand pills and a pair of weighing scales.
Hunter?
…
Mate, these modern jails
All look the fuckin' same,
But this old lockup,
You can still make out where Kenno scratched his
fuckin' name
On my first day, he bashed shit out of Shelton after a
game
Of two-up. Musta been Anzac Day.

Are ya gone?

And bullet hole here, see? From when young Col went
nuts?

Turned up with his shirt ripped open, fuckin' cuts all
over his body,
Stopped off at the bakery, picked up his old man's shottie,
Just went crazy, you remember?
Hunter?

Or remember those bozos who come in from the city to
shoot roos?
In their shitty four-wheel drives, so fuckin' fulla smoke
and booze
That all they ended up shootin' was each other?
I found this here, see? The card that his mother wrote me.

He takes a card from one of the boxes.

Kid sat right there and he just bled to death,
Bullet hole through his jaw, smell of beer still on his
breath,
His brother screamin' murder, off his head on crystal
meth,
It was terrible, Jesus it was a terrible night.
[*Reading*] 'I find comfort that yours was the last face he
saw
Before he closed his eyes forever
And was met by the Lord', see?
…
Don't know what kinda fuckin' state he was in when
they met.

And you know what I was thinkin'?
I was thinkin' 'bout that night.
Joey Slater for a DUI, and Sweeney for a fist fight.
Put 'em both in the same lockup, well they musta got on
alright,
'Cause Sweeney left his missus
And they both moved up to Sydney two weeks later.

Who'd have thought it?
Hunter?

Joey fuckin' Slater!

And you know they say that walls have ears? I reckon
that it's true.
And late at night, after a few beers, they start talking to
you,
And they remind ya of all the lives that made their way
through this place.
Half of 'em are dead, mate.
Half of 'em are dead.
…
Like Coops.
He's fuckin' dead.
Shot his own dog, mate, shot him through the head
Before he turned it on himself.
Everybody said it was the drought.
It fuckin' wasn't the drought.
…
The thing is, Hunter, what I'm tryin' to say …
…
Is you don't just walk …
You don't just leave …
Hunter?
…
It just woulda been impossible for me to stay.

SCENE FIVE

Margaret's flat.
It is dark. There is a knock on the door.

HUNTER: [*from outside*] Mum?
RADIO: You're listening to 'Night Talk' …
HUNTER: Mum?
RADIO: On AM Radio 314.
HUNTER: Mum?
MARGARET: Who is it?

HUNTER: Well, obviously it's me, Mum.

MARGARET: Who?

HUNTER: Me! Will you open up the door?!

MARGARET: Graham?

HUNTER: Open up the door.

MARGARET switches off the radio. Opens the door. HUNTER
enters.

MARGARET: Is it time to go?

HUNTER: What?

MARGARET: Is it time to go back?

HUNTER: Where?

MARGARET: To the house.
            I think I need more time, Graham.
            I don't know how I'm meant to pack.
            I don't know where I'm meant to start.

HUNTER: Mum.

MARGARET: It's all just … I don't know if I can.

HUNTER: Can you turn on the fucking lights at least?
            It's like a—

MARGARET: Language!

Lights come on. MARGARET *is in a dressing-gown and looks a
little worse for wear.*

            I've forgotten what was mine and what was here.
            I don't know if I need bedsheets,
            Or cutlery, or underwear.

HUNTER: It's alright …

MARGARET: I woke up and I thought that I was in my old room,
            But I'd shrunk, to a tiny …
            The size of a dog.

HUNTER: A dog?

MARGARET: A doll! The size of a doll. Just small.
            I kept getting lost and I thought I would fall
            Through the cracks in the floor.

HUNTER: It's your tablets, Mum.

MARGARET: I don't know …

HUNTER: It's alright.

MARGARET: I just don't know if I can anymore.

HUNTER: It's alright, Mum!

MARGARET: I'm sorry, Graham.

HUNTER: Shhh.

                   …
                   You know I'd never ask you to do anything you didn't
                   want to do,
                   Would I?
                   Mum?

MARGARET: Hmm?

HUNTER: Would I?

MARGARET: Oh, no.

HUNTER: You know that whatever you decided,
                   That I'd support you?
                   Don't you?
                   Mum?

MARGARET: Hmm?

HUNTER: You know that, don't you?

MARGARET: Oh, yes.

                   …

HUNTER: If you wanted to go back, then I'd support that too,
                   But if you wanted to stay, then I'd make sure that you—

MARGARET: [*suddenly suspicious*] What's going on, Graham?

HUNTER: Nothing.

                   …
                   You want a cup of tea?

MARGARET: At this hour?

HUNTER: It's hardly—

MARGARET: Brandy. I'll have a brandy.

HUNTER: Where am I supposed to get—?

MARGARET: Under the sink.

HUNTER *goes.* MARGARET *does herself up as best she can and* HUNTER *returns with a bottle of brandy and two glasses. He pours.*

HUNTER: Dad liked a brandy.

MARGARET: Your father liked anything so long as it was wet.

          Silence.

HUNTER: I probably got that from him. Mum?

MARGARET: Hmm?

HUNTER: I probably—

MARGARET: Maybe.

HUNTER: Cheers.

          …

          What else did I get from him, do you reckon?

MARGARET: Hmm?

HUNTER: What else did I get from Dad?

MARGARET: What?

HUNTER: Nose? Ears?

MARGARET: Where is this going, Graham?

HUNTER: Nowhere. Just. I'm wondering what traits I got from Dad.

MARGARET: Traits?

HUNTER: You know. Things.

MARGARET: Things? You got plenty of things from Dad, Graham.

HUNTER: Like?

MARGARET: Like you both ask ridiculous questions for a start.

HUNTER: He was my father though, right?

MARGARET: What? Of course he was your father.

HUNTER: And Gordon?

MARGARET: I beg your pardon? I think you've lost your mind.

HUNTER: Was Gordon …?

MARGARET: Of course Gordon was!

HUNTER: Mum.

MARGARET: I will not be held to scrutiny in my own home!

GORDON: Mum?!

GORDON *comes in with* RACHEL.

You got the front door wide open …
[*Seeing* HUNTER] What are you doing here?

MARGARET: Oh yes, that's right! *That's right!*
The three of us together after how many years?
And all I get is nonsense, and 'What are you doing here's?'.
I've had enough. Go!

GORDON: You been gettin' her pissed?

MARGARET: I will not have that language! Go!

RACHEL: Margaret …

MARGARET: No! No, I'm sorry, Rachel, I insist that you all leave now!
This instant!

She turns away from them.

Silence. They all look at her.

She turns back.

You're all still here.

HUNTER: Mum, we want to ask you something.

GORDON: We know.

MARGARET: Know? What? Nothing!

GORDON: About Dad. About us.

MARGARET: You wouldn't have a clue.
You wouldn't have the foggiest about anything.
I've had enough. The lot of you.
Get out!

GORDON: Mum, there's been a blood test.

MARGARET *is speechless.*

Mum?

HUNTER: Mum.

RACHEL: Margaret …

GORDON: Mum, listen. This is really important.
We need to know which one of us is actually Dad's real son.

…

HUNTER: Mum?

RACHEL: Margaret?

GORDON: Mum, listen, it's really important. We need know which
             one—

MARGARET: *I'll tell you what is really important.*
             Raising a healthy family, *that's* what's important!
             Putting food on the table again and again and again,
             Keeping a family together, *that's* what's important!

RACHEL: No-one is saying—

MARGARET: Yes they are! That's exactly what they're saying!
             Keeping a family of three grown men
             From killing each other!
             That's what's important!
             ...

HUNTER: Mum—

MARGARET: A family is more than eggs and seed!

GORDON: [*shocked and disgusted in equal measure*] Oh, Mum.

HUNTER: [*equally so*] Jesus Christ.

MARGARET: A family is something that happens to people,
             It isn't something you pick up and read
             From a blood test?! For goodness sake. A blood test? I
             ask you!
             It's something you love and you clothe and you feed,
             It's not something—

HUNTER: *Fucking hell!*
             Why didn't you tell us?!

MARGARET: *You?!* You'd be the last person I'd tell.
             The pair of you?
             You'd be the last people I'd tell.
             ...
             It was different.
             It was a different time.

HUNTER: It was back then,
             But Jesus, Mum,
             We're both grown men,
             I mean, why didn't you ...?

MARGARET: It was a different time!

    …

    I tried,
    But things got in the way, and then after Dad died …
    It seemed less important.

    …

GORDON: So one of us—

MARGARET: If you say so.

HUNTER: It's possible though?

MARGARET: Yes!

    …

GORDON: And?

MARGARET: And what?

    …

                   Nobody loved you any less … Gordon.

GORDON: Oh, my God. Did he know?

MARGARET: I don't think so.

GORDON: But he might of?

    …

MARGARET: Nobody loved you any less.

  Silence.

HUNTER: Dad left the land to *his* children and *his* grandchildren—

RACHEL: Hunter, don't!

    …

GORDON: [*to* HUNTER] If you put her up to this, I'll fucking—

MARGARET: Language!

RACHEL: Sweetheart, maybe we should—

GORDON: *No!*

    If you put her up to this, I swear to God …

    …

RACHEL: Gordon. It's time to go.

  GORDON *leaves.* RACHEL *looks at both* HUNTER *and*
  MARGARET *and follows.*

MARGARET: 'Put me up to it.' Who does he think I am?

HUNTER: It's alright, Mum.

MARGARET: As if it's not—

HUNTER: It's alright, Mum.
             It's a shock.

MARGARET: I know it's a shock. It's a shock to me.
             …
             I never meant—

HUNTER: Of course not, Mum.

MARGARET: I always tried—

HUNTER: I know.

MARGARET: It's family, son … You wouldn't understand.

        They look at each other.

        It's time for you to go.

SCENE SIX

MARGARET *and* RACHEL *speak directly to the audience.*

MARGARET: It was before the boys were born that I—

RACHEL: Before the girls were born, I remember I—

MARGARET: Took a train alone to the city—

RACHEL: Used to pretty much write myself off every /
                 weekend …

MARGARET: / There were tests that they needed done.

RACHEL: Drinking West Coast Cooler until / closing

MARGARET: / And I stayed with my half-deaf aunt in a little townhouse
             in Abbotsford.
             I think it was Connolly Street.

RACHEL: The pub was called the Shearer's Arse.

MARGARET: O' Connolly Street?

RACHEL: It was the Shearer's Arms but the 'M' had fallen off.

MARGARET: McConnelly Street?

RACHEL: I used to meet the girls beforehand,
             We'd do our hair and drink shots of vodka

Before heading out to the Shearer's.

MARGARET: A girl I knew from high school—

RACHEL: God, I shudder to think of *my* girls at that age.

MARGARET: Was nursing at the Alfred.

RACHEL: Oh my God, they almost are, you know.

MARGARET: Not where the tests were being done,
              But for some company and just for fun
              We met for a drink at a nearby hotel.

RACHEL: But best not to think about that till you have to.

MARGARET: And she introduced me to a friend of hers,
              A doctor.

RACHEL: A doctor?

MARGARET: Hmm.

RACHEL: The boys would come in after football.

MARGARET: A doctor.

RACHEL: All Winfield Reds and Manage aftershave,
              Jugs of beer to drink their brains away,
              Shots of Bunderburg OP
              And see who'd be the first to spew.

MARGARET: So unlike any of the other boys I knew in Cradletown.

RACHEL: Some of the girls had boyfriends.

MARGARET: Of course I was seeing Graham already.

RACHEL: They talked about the boys or to the boys
              Or cried in the loo to their best friends about what pricks
              they were …

MARGARET: We had been courting for about a year.

RACHEL: And some of the girls dreamt of love …

MARGARET: And my parents thought he was lovely.

RACHEL: But not many.

MARGARET: No?

RACHEL: [*shaking her head*] Not many.
              …

As far as I knew, every love story
Ended in violence or alimony payments
Or both.

MARGARET: Graham was very much the gentleman.

RACHEL: Usually both.

MARGARET: Just not when he was drinking.

RACHEL: And I just knew that it wasn't for me.
I wanted a good man and I wanted stability.
And I knew—

MARGARET: The only doctor I'd met before
Was Dr Cole and he was seventy-four in the shade.

RACHEL: —that that's what I wanted.

MARGARET: And certainly didn't wear *eau de Cologne*.

RACHEL: And I got what I wanted.

MARGARET: He told me he would walk me home,
He said a girl in a strange town on her own
Could get into trouble.

RACHEL: Not to say I lived like a nun.

MARGARET: I thought it was a figure of speech!

RACHEL: Not to say I didn't have my share of fun.

MARGARET: He put his coat around my shoulders
Put his arm around me
And said, 'Trust me, I'm a doctor'.

RACHEL: Oh, I had my share of fun.

MARGARET: We walked two suburbs home
While the streets were being cleaned.
… I'd never seen streets being cleaned before,
It sounds ridiculous.

RACHEL: Sometimes I look at the girls in their beds
And I think of the dreams going on in their heads
And I cry.

MARGARET: I don't know how I thought streets got clean.

RACHEL: I just cry.

MARGARET: And I don't know why but for some reason,
                     I thought that he could bring me luck,
                     For my tests the next day.
                     I felt deeply that if I embraced this moment
                     Then the tests would go well.
                     And if they didn't,
                     Then at least … I had embraced the moment.
                     And I did.

                     In the front room of my aunt's little townhouse in
                     Abbotsford.
                     And he was a perfect gentleman.
                     And he kissed me on the lips when he left.
                     And he told me to stay warm.
                     …
                     Thank God my aunt was half-deaf.
                     …
                     Thank God there were tests that I needed done.

RACHEL: The dog brought a dead bird in from the garden
                     And we buried it in the backyard and
                     Gracie kept saying we were planting it—
MARGARET: I came back home and everything was fine—
RACHEL: She thought we were *planting* the bird.
MARGARET: Things went back to normal, the tests were benign.
RACHEL: And then two weeks later—
MARGARET: And then two weeks later I told Graham
                     That if he proposed to me, I'd say yes.
                     And he did.
                     …
                     And we did.
                     …
RACHEL: Two weeks later, Gracie ran in to tell us
                     To look outside, as a flock of rosellas

Were flying up from the horizon.
She said, 'I told you so,
That bird that we planted grew into new ones'.

RACHEL *and* MARGARET *look at each other and smile.*

SCENE SEVEN

It is some weeks later.

GORDON *and* RACHEL *are outside not far from the old house.* GORDON *is reading from a glossy real estate brochure.* RACHEL *is calling to the girls, who are offstage.*

GORDON: [*reading*] Idyllic Open Spaces!
RACHEL: [*to the girls offstage*] Hold your grandma's hand, sweetheart!
GORDON: In an Impressive Landscape Setting.
RACHEL: Gracie! Hold on!
GORDON: Enjoy the Complete Living Experience
Home and Land Packages now being offered
In the beautiful Lakes Residential Estate,
Stage One now selling.
Rachel?
RACHEL: Hmm?
GORDON: It's got an artist's impression too,
See?
RACHEL: [*to the girls*] Nice and slowly, that's it sweetheart!
GORDON: It's amazing what they can do. See?
RACHEL: Why is it called the Lakes Residential?
There isn't a lake.
GORDON: There's the dam.
RACHEL: Well, shouldn't it be called the damn residential estate?
GORDON: That's not funny or helpful, Rachel.
Are the girls okay?
RACHEL: They're with Margaret.
GORDON: I can't see them.
RACHEL: Let them be.

GORDON: [*calling out*] Mum!

RACHEL: Let them be!

GORDON: I am letting them—

RACHEL: Let her say goodbye.

     Pause.

     Jacaranda's finished for another year.

GORDON: [*not looking up*] Mhmm.

RACHEL: A few weeks' blossom's all they have.
     Six weeks at most, from bloom to broom,
     Is that what they say? Or rake I suppose.
     Is it coming down?

GORDON: What?

RACHEL: The jacaranda tree. Are they chopping it down?

GORDON: I expect so. I don't know.

RACHEL: Well, is it in the artist's impression?

GORDON: [*looking*] Nope.

     Pause.

RACHEL: You should take some time to say goodbye as well.
     You'll miss it when it's gone.

GORDON: It's not going anywhere, Rachel.
     Land doesn't just go.
     It changes.
     It develops.
     That's why it's called a development.

RACHEL: Is that why?

GORDON: A-huh.
     It looked different a hundred years ago,
     It'll look different a hundred years from now,
     You and I are just passing through.

RACHEL: Well, Gordon, as we do, let's stop and
     And say goodbye.

GORDON: I've said goodbye.

     He looks up.

Goodbye house.
Even though I moved out twenty years ago, goodbye.
Goodbye dam. Goodbye yard.
Goodbye Etho.

RACHEL: Etho?

GORDON: Just something silly.
What me and Hunter used to call it.

RACHEL: Etho?

GORDON: Hmm.

RACHEL: Why?

GORDON: I don't know—
I can't remember.

They look out. Lights are gradually changing to evening.

Mum's taking the girls to the tree.
When Dad died, she planted a tree,
I'd forgotten about that.
…
Have the girls got a jacket? Are they—?

RACHEL: They're fine.

Pause.

GORDON: You hear that?

RACHEL: What?

GORDON: Trucks.
You can hear them going down Wiseman's Bend,
If they take it too fast they slam on the breaks and send
That smell of burning right across town, you know?
They're gettin' ready to start work in the morning.
…
You remember that livestock truck took it too fast
And he rolled and his pigs all went head over arse
And went scrambling like crazy up Old Wiseman's
Track?
They searched all arvo, only got half of 'em back.
…
The town was eating pork for a week.

They look out. GORDON *refers back to his brochure.*

	It says of fourteen lots
	Ranging from one thousand to sixteen hundred square feet.
	I can't quite make out the plan,
	But I think this'll be Chardonnay Street
	Running all the way down to the old orchard.
	And that'll be Primrose Crescent.
	You see?
	And there's a recreational reserve.
RACHEL:	Where?
GORDON:	Out by the Wheelers' property, I suppose.
	I don't know, it just says it's proposed somewhere in Stage Three.
	See?
	And guess what they're calling Dead Man's Rise?
RACHEL:	What?
GORDON:	Hunter's Hill.
RACHEL:	*No!*
GORDON:	That's what it says.
	[*Reading*] 'Undulating Hunter's Hill
	Offers lots that gently spill
	Into the surrounding farmland.'
RACHEL:	Sounds like a sewerage problem.
GORDON:	We used to slide down there on sheets of tin,
	I hit a tree and got a lump on my shin
	The size of a tennis ball.
	…
	Hunter's Hill.
RACHEL:	He might see the irony.
GORDON:	I'm not sure he will.
RACHEL:	When do you think he'll—?
GORDON:	I don't know.
	…
	He said it won't be seven years.
	He said he'd stay in touch.

He said that he'd be back
But that he couldn't bear to watch.
…
That's all he said.

They look out.

It's really going, isn't it?

RACHEL: I believe so.
…
Why don't you say goodbye.

GORDON: What do you want me to do? Sing a song?
…
Goodbye!
Goodbye Etho!

He waves and looks as if suddenly seeing it for the first time.

Goodbye.

MARGARET: [*from offstage*] Yes alright! We're coming!

GORDON: No, I wasn't! … I was just—

RACHEL: Gracie! Take your things off Grandma, she's not a camel!
Well, carry them yourself!
Margaret, just give them back to her!
Coralie! What have you done with your shoes?
I swear to God, those girls.

She goes.

GORDON: [*to himself*] I was just saying goodbye.

He looks out. He closes his eyes. He opens them.

MARGARET *enters.*

How were they, Mum?

MARGARET: They were fine. They just put their feet in the dam.

GORDON: There's an eel down there still plotting revenge.

MARGARET: We only stood by the edge.

GORDON: They could have slipped.

MARGARET: And what? Been eaten by an eel?

GORDON: I'm just saying …

MARGARET: I swear, those girls are terrified of anything that doesn't
tweet or twitter.

GORDON: It's slippery.

MARGARET: Dad threw you boys in that dam when you were half
their age.

GORDON: Well, we prefer to give the girls swimming lessons.

MARGARET: Coralie said, 'We can't take off our shoes, we might
catch cold'.
What is she? Sixty?

GORDON: She knows she's not supposed to—

MARGARET: You boys rode bikes without helmets,
You swum in the dam,
You had fireworks and bonfires,
You turned out alright.

GORDON: I seem to remember Matt McCoy lost his finger one
cracker night, Mum.

MARGARET: Oh, he would have lost that anyway—

GORDON: Times have / changed /

MARGARET: / If ever there was a boy
Who was going to lose a finger, it was Matt McCoy!
He would have lost it in the bath.

GORDON: Well, the girls aren't—

MARGARET: They can do with a little more time outside,
That's all I'm saying.

GORDON: Well, maybe you can see to that.

MARGARET: I will. I am.
Graham said I should take a more active part in their
upbringing.

GORDON: I know he did.

MARGARET: He said a grandmother has a right to see her
grandchildren.

GORDON: I know, Mum, I know he did.

MARGARET: Gracie wants a horse.

GORDON: A pony, Mum, and we said we'd see.

MARGARET: She said that you—

GORDON: And she
Can't just blink her eyes and expect ponies to appear.

MARGARET: It's a shame I don't live here anymore,
It would have been perfect for a horse.

GORDON: Well, you just don't.

                …

There's nothing in the house now, Mum?

MARGARET: It's all cleared out.

GORDON: You know it's coming down.

MARGARET: It'll look strange without a house anymore.

GORDON: There'll be sixteen new ones built before
You know it.

                …

Will you miss it?

MARGARET: Missing things is for the young.
Old people can't afford to miss things too much,
There'd be no end to it if we did.
Will you?

Pause.

I will miss it, but what can you do?
Young people need somewhere to live too.

She takes his arm. It is almost completely dusk. RACHEL *re-enters.*

RACHEL: The girls are in the car!

The three stand and look out.

Margaret, will you come to our place for tea?

MARGARET: If I can—

RACHEL: Gordon can run you home? Can't you, Gordon?

GORDON: Apparently.

                …

MARGARET: I'll never get tired of that view.

They all look out.

GORDON: Let's go.

RACHEL: We can try our new electric wok frying pan.

GORDON: We picked it up on credit points.
            Visa card credit points, didn't we sweetheart?
            It's amazing. It's an electric wok,
            The stir-fry tosses itself. It's better than Chinese.
            You put your vegies in and you … the smell is amazing

The three go.

SCENE EIGHT

GORDON *returns on stage.* HUNTER *comes from the opposite side.*
They speak directly to the audience.

GORDON: Mum had this thing about fumes
            And she used to lock us both in our rooms
            When we were making model aeroplanes,
            She said it interfered with our brains
            And so her answer was to lock us in the only room that
            didn't have a window.

HUNTER: So we're sitting there, the two of us
            With model planes and glue and us two
            Trying to connect section 12 to 3-1-2,
            And Gordon looks across at me and just goes, 'I dare ya',
            And I look back and go, 'I fuckin' dare you!'

GORDON: And I dab a bit of glue just on my fingers and my palm,
            But then Hunter grabs the tube and squeezes it up right
            my arm,
            And the next thing I know he's fucking gluing my
            pyjamas to my shoulder.
            And I grab him—

HUNTER: Gordon's bigger, and he's older—

GORDON: And I put our arms together and refuse to let them go!

HUNTER: And then by the time he does,
            Ya fuckin' nong!

GORDON: Our skin's fully glued from our hands, all along right to
            our elbow.

HUNTER: Ya dick!
           …
           And we panic and we're pulling and we just fall to the
           ground—
GORDON: 'Cause it's both of our left arms and we're just goin'
           round and round
           In fuckin' circles for an hour.
HUNTER: And I push him down the stairs.
GORDON: But he comes flyin' after me
           And almost tears the skin right off our arm.
HUNTER: Fuck, it hurt!
GORDON: And Mum, she says nothing, she just makes us eat our tea,
           With our arms across the table,
           Hunter's staring at me, like he wants to kill me,
           And then Mum just makes us go to bed.
HUNTER: And there was almost bloodshed that night.
           Almost bloodshed.
           …
           Mum wouldn't believe us how much it fucking hurt.
GORDON: And she reckoned that we had to go to school the next
           day!
HUNTER: Which was bullshit because neither of us could put on
           our school shirt.
GORDON: And I was still glued into my pyjama top anyway.
HUNTER: So we wagged the day in Etho.
GORDON: Wagged the next two days.
HUNTER: Just sittin' there, talking.
GORDON: Looking out—
HUNTER: —opposite ways—
GORDON: —over Etho.
HUNTER: Just talking about any old shit.
           Eatin' our school sandwiches and tryin' to hit the eel
           with rocks.
GORDON: Three days just stuck together.
           Eatin', sleepin', talkin' or whatever.

HUNTER: Takin' a crap.

GORDON: And then on the third day, we feel the glue give way,
            And slowly we feel our arms peeling apart.

HUNTER: But neither of us actually says anything—

GORDON: And we just keep sittin' there till it's dark.

HUNTER: And then just make our way home.
            Neither of us says nothin'.

            …

GORDON: And then later we're sittin' either side of our room,
            Just lyin' there pickin' off the last bits of the glue.
            And Hunter goes to me, 'I can still feel ya'

HUNTER: And Gordon goes—

GORDON: Yeah, I can still feel you too.

They walk off in opposite directions.

Lights out.

THE END